JESUS IS RISEN
Theology for the Church

The Lifework and Teaching of
The Rev. Dr. Walter R. Bouman, ThD

VOLUME 1

ANN M. HAUT, EDITOR

Lutheran University Press
Minneapolis, Minnesota

JESUS IS RISEN

Theology for the Church

The Lifework and Teaching of The Rev. Dr. Walter R. Bouman, ThD

VOLUME 1

Ann M. Haut, editor

ISBN: 978-1-942304-02-9

Lutheran University Press, PO Box 390759, Minneapolis, MN 55439
www.lutheranupress.org
Printed in the United States of America

For Jan, of course,
with love.
Walt

TABLE OF CONTENTS

Introduction 7

CHAPTER 1
The Good News of the Church 11

CHAPTER 2
The Confession That Jesus Is God 35

CHAPTER 3
The Historical Mission of Jesus 53

CHAPTER 4
The *Skandalon* of the Cross: The Crucified Messiah 75

CHAPTER 5
The Resurrection of Jesus as the Power of the Future 107

CHAPTER 6
The Suffering of God 131

CHAPTER 7
The Holy Spirit 149

CHAPTER 8
The Trinity and Language for God 165

Endnotes 184

Bibliography 201

INTRODUCTION

Walter R. Bouman was the Edward C. Fendt Professor of Systematic Theology at Trinity Lutheran Seminary from 1971 to 2005. He was thoroughly devoted to the church, to its people and especially to his students. His curriculum vitae featured long lists of lectures, presentations, and sermons he delivered throughout his career. He taught and preached the Word of God around the globe—from Holden Village in the North Range of the Cascade Mountains of Washington to New York City, from small towns in Australia to tiny villages in Africa and on to cities of Europe. Face-to-face interaction energized him. When he retired, he worried that he might be forgotten or ignored, and that the telephone would cease to ring. In fact, it never stopped ringing.

Throughout his tenure at Trinity, scores of Dr. Bouman's students encouraged him to write a book that they might share with the members of their congregations. When he learned that he had terminal cancer in April 2005, he realized he never would write that book. In May he asked me to take on the task.

He directed that the book's readership should be members of congregations and entry-level seminary students. He dictated its outline and directed materials from lectures that he wanted to be included. He read drafts of early chapters until his energy would no longer allow him to focus. When he could do no more, he offered the words for the dedication page: *For Jan, of course, with love.*

These two volumes are based on transcribed tapes and outlines from his 1992-93 lectures, referred to in the seminary course catalog as HTS 1041 and HTS 1042. As a student who sat through those lectures, I worked to retain cherished stories and examples. My own goals in this writing were to be true to Dr. Bouman's essential messages, and then to reflect his voice in the way that his message is conveyed. I hope that persons who knew him well will hear him echoing in their memories as they read this text.

Six of Dr. Bouman's students read and edited these pages before they were submitted to the publisher. Thanks be to God for the many gifts of commentary offered by the Rev. Luke Bouman; the Rev. Al Debelak of Redeemer Lutheran Church in Columbus, Ohio; the Rev. Vicki Garber of Gloria Dei Lutheran Church in Crestview Hills, Kentucky; the Rev. Dr. Anna M. Madsen of OMG: Center for Theological Conversation, Sioux Falls, South Dakota; the Rev. Timothy Muller of Ascension Lutheran Church in Columbus, Ohio; and the Rev. Rebecca Robbins-Penniman of The Church of the Good Shepherd in Dunedin, Florida.

All proceeds from these volumes are donated to the Walter R. and Janet A. Bouman Chair of Church Music at Trinity Lutheran Seminary.

Finally, just as Dr. Bouman closed all of his letters and emails, this introduction also concludes: Peace and non-violence.

Ann Marie Haut, PhD

The Rev. Dr. Walter R. Bouman

SEVEN STANZAS AT EASTER[1]

by John Updike

Make no mistake: if He rose at all
it was as His body;
if the cells' dissolution did not reverse, the molecules reknit,
    the amino acids rekindle,
the Church will fall.

It was not as the flowers,
each soft Spring recurrent;
it was not as His Spirit in the mouths and fuddled eyes of the
    eleven apostles;
it was as His Flesh: ours.

The same hinged thumbs and toes,
the same valved heart
that—pierced—died, withered, paused, and then regathered
    out of enduring Might
new strength to enclose.

Let us not mock God with metaphor,
analogy, sidestepping transcendence;
making of the event a parable, a sign painted in the faded
    credulity of earlier ages:
let us walk through the door.

The stone is rolled back, not papier-mâché,
not a stone in a story,
but the vast rock of materiality that in the slow grinding of
    time will eclipse for each of us
the wide light of day.

And if we will have an angel at the tomb,
make it a real angel,
weighty with Max Planck's quanta, vivid with hair, opaque in
    the dawn light, robed in real linen
spun on a definite loom.

Let us not seek to make it less monstrous,
for our own convenience, our own sense of beauty,
lest, awakened in one unthinkable hour, we are embarrassed
    by the miracle,
and crushed by remonstrance.

CHAPTER 1

THE GOOD NEWS OF THE CHURCH

The Christian Gospel is the good news that Jesus is risen. It was the disciples' earliest good news, and it continues to be the good news of the church today.

The reason why the Gospel was and is *news* is that it describes an important event—a resurrection—which had never happened before. And it has not happened since.

On one level, we must say that the resurrection is important because it vindicated (or showed to be righteous) everything about Jesus: If Jesus is resurrected, it is because God did it. Therefore, in Jesus' resurrection, God affirms all that Jesus had been saying, doing, and claiming.

On another level, the resurrection is good news because through it the disciples encountered Jesus as Messiah. True, they spent years following Jesus throughout Israel. True, they heard his parables and his announcement of the nearness of God's kingdom. And true, they sought his counsel and his favor. However, in all of these occasions and circumstances, never had they truly understood who Jesus was or what he was doing. Until the resurrection. The resurrection changed everything then, and it still changes everything now—and that is why it is still "news."

We know from the apostle Paul that "if Christ has not been raised, then our proclamation has been in vain and your faith has been in vain" (1 Corinthians 15:14). Here Paul addresses concerns of some people of that era—and indeed, some people who still may wonder—if the resurrection of Jesus was only a ruse. Was it just a story? Indeed, detractors have offered at least four challenges to the historicity of the resurrection event, among them, suppositions that: a) Jesus was not dead when he was buried; b) the disciples borrowed non-Jewish stories of dying and rising gods, and adapted these stories to accommodate Jesus' resurrection; c) a change occurred in the hearts of the disciples, who turned a tragic death into a heroic vision; or d) the disciples experienced hallucinations.[2]

How are we to evaluate critics' variations in the Christ event? Wolfhart Pannenberg says that "in being a Christian, everything depends on the reality of God. We cannot honestly go on to identify ourselves as Christians if the story of Jesus Christ and of his God is merely a story (in the sense of fairy tale)—fiction, but not history. . . . The story of Jesus Christ has to be history, not in all its details, but in its core, if the Christian faith is to continue."[3]

Rooted in biblical narrative, the four Gospels maintain remarkable consistency regarding the disciples' reaction to both Jesus' crucifixion and resurrection. Jesus died a shameful death on a cross—and in the shadow of that cross, the disciples fled in utter disarray. However, a short time later they returned to Jerusalem and began to proclaim that Jesus was the Messiah. Clearly, the Gospel authors believed that something *happened* between the disciples' flight from Jesus' crucifixion and their joyous return to the city. Biblical texts are consistent in their reports that that "something" was Jesus' resurrection.

The point must be made that the resurrection of Jesus was an event: It occurred in history, in a particular place and at a particular time. That is, it happened; it is real. Here we are making the point that the Gospel is not first of all about an *idea*—for example, the idea that God loves the world, even though that idea is true; rather, the Gospel is about an *event*. Furthermore, to announce that it happened and to have that announcement make sense is what makes it "news." Because the event is essential to the root meaning of Gospel, it is then correctly referred to as "good news." And because it continues to be new information to people who have yet to hear its truth (that is, to recognize the resurrection as an event and then to interpret its impact with regard to how they understand God's participation in human history), it continues to be "news."

The earliest written witness (that is, the first recorded "news") to the resurrection is found in 1 Corinthians 15:3-8. This letter to the church in Corinth is dated 52 A.D.; the opening text, however ("For I handed on to you as of first importance what I in turn had received . . ."), suggests that Paul preserved language which was likely to have originated within months, or at most a couple of years, after Jesus' resurrection. In this way, he retains the earlier, existing witness upon which he relied, thereby lending credibility to his assertions.

Paul's letter provides readers in Corinth (and us today) with a brief synopsis of the passion story and its following witness: Jesus died, was buried, and on the third day was raised; he then appeared to Cephas, to the remaining disciples, and finally to more than 500 others.[4] It is understood, therefore, that these people were available to share their witness, should anyone care to ask them about their encounters with Jesus. Furthermore, Paul's letter to the people of Corinth shows that "resurrection" was an accepted tenet of the Jewish faith.

We also need to say that Jesus' resurrection was not a resuscitation. That is, following his resurrection Jesus did not resume a life in which he was still subject to death. He had transcended death, and he was no longer subject to its power. As we know from Romans 6:9, "We know that Christ, being raised from the dead, will never die again; death no longer has dominion over him."

The task. In this chapter, we begin with thoughts about the theology of the church—ideas about meaning and about authority, about coherence, about truthfulness and plausibility—which give us a basis for the things we are going to say in this book. With these thoughts in mind, we can discuss why understanding the resurrection of Jesus as "news" is meaningful for us today. We will discuss how the disciples reacted as they did at the cross, and the importance of their return when the event of the resurrection opened their eyes to what God was doing—and is doing—in the world. In this, we will grasp the essence of God's radical "yes!" toward all creation.

The Church's Theology

The task of theology is truth. As people who live in the midst of a culturally powerful secularity and post-modern pluralist religiosity,[5] the question of truth is not an easy one.

The church's theology informs how its theological teachers—that is, persons charged by their ordination and persons charged by their commissioning—attend to the truthfulness upon which the church proclaims, teaches, and lives its story. Members of congregations also attend to this truth; here we are attempting to clarify how to better grasp it. This undertaking involves three dimensions: the meaning of language, authority, and coherence.

Meaning of language. The words and phrases commonly used by teachers of the church's theology must have common understandings. That is, language must be publicly intelligible so that, for example, when we say "God" we know about whom or what we are speaking. Here we might want to refer to a delightful statement by C.S. Lewis:

> If you do not listen to Theology, that will not mean that you have no ideas about God. It will mean that you have a lot of wrong ones—bad, muddled, out-of-date ideas. For a great many of the ideas which are trotted out as novelties today are simply the ones which real theologians tried centuries ago and rejected. To believe in the popular religion of modern England is a retrogression—like believing the earth is flat. . . .

> For when you get down to it, is not the popular idea of Christianity simply this: that Jesus Christ was a great moral teacher and that if only we took his advice we might be able to establish a better social order and avoid another war?

> But as soon as you look at any real Christian writings, you find that they are talking about something quite different from this popular religion. They say that Christ is the Son of God (whatever that means). They say that those who give Him their confidence can also become Sons of God

(whatever that means). . . . It is no good complaining that these statements are difficult. You may think the Christian claim false; but if it were true, what it tells us would be bound to be difficult—at least as difficult as modern Physics, and for the same reason. . . .

If Christianity was something we were making up, of course we could make it easier. But it is not. We cannot compete, in simplicity, with people who are inventing religions. How could we? We are dealing with Fact. Of course anyone can be simple if he has no facts to bother about.[6]

C.S. Lewis was speaking about how people in the United Kingdom thought about "God" in the mid-twentieth century—and the same thing can be still be said in both the U.K. and in the United States today. One of the great problems with our public language is that the word "God" is used without specificity, as if everyone knows what we have in mind. But that is not the case. Do we have in mind Benjamin Franklin's understanding of God? Or Thomas Jefferson's idea? Or Mary Baker Eddy's perspective? The Christian Trinity? The Jewish understanding? We must specify with great clarity what we mean. I want to say that theology is required to identify concrete sensory meanings for its terms and claims. We must share a common language for what we mean when we make a claim.

Again, we are saying here that Jesus of Nazareth, born of Mary and executed under Pontius Pilate, Roman procurator of Judea from 26 to 36 A.D., is God. The events of his life and death occurred in and are recorded in history. We know they are true. And this truth contains *meaning* for us, then and today. That meaning is this: Jesus is God.

Authority. Secondly, attention must be given to the *grounding* or *authority* for the church's language. The term "grounding" refers to providing adequate or plausible reasons for meanings or explanations which are proposed and claims which are advanced. For example, if I say to you, "God means blue cheese," I have asserted a meaningful statement—that is, a statement which *means* something. It may or may not be adequate or plausible, but now we can have a conversation about that. While you are momentarily surprised by my assertion, when you pause to think about it, you can conjure up an image in your mind of blue cheese: crumbling, gorgeous, smelly blue cheese! You may have doubts about whether or not you want to worship with me, but you will be under no illusions about what I mean! So I have made a *meaningful* statement. And you could then say, "On what grounds do you, Walter Bouman, assert that 'God means blue cheese'?" That is, "*Why* do you say that?"

"I like it," I'd respond.

You'd say, "Well, that is indeed a reason, but it is not adequate because not everything that a person likes can be used to complete the statement, 'God means—.'"

Do you see? The moment that you lay this out and make an assertion of what God means, the question, "Why do you say that?" can be addressed. And then we can start looking at the adequacy of both your reason and the meaning you have proposed. So adequate grounding or authority for what we mean is the second dimension.

We are going to say that the One who has been resurrected from death—the One over whom death has no power—is God. This means Jesus is God.

Coherence. Thirdly, we must give attention to the coherence of the church's language. "Coherence" means that the church's specific story is consistent in three ways:

- Consistent within itself: If I say something about the meaning of God, I must be able to connect it to the sacraments, for example. If God means blue cheese, then why are we bothering with bread and wine? Why not blue cheese and Scotch whiskey? So one set of meanings must cohere with other sets of meanings, and there must be some way to fit them all together.

- Consistent with the way in which we understand the world: We want to avoid compartmentalizing. Compartmentalizing can happen if we have private language for Sunday morning or for when we pray—but the words and phrases we use don't have anything to do with banking or driving an automobile or owning property or voting on Tuesday, or indeed, anything else. Integrity in the use of language requires consistency in the ways in which we use words. Coherence requires that our participation in the larger world make sense in light of what we do on Sunday morning.

- Consistent with expectations of justice, compassion, and hope which are characteristic of the reign of God: One can make up a plausible account of Christianity that would leave us defenseless before an Adolph Hitler—but such an account would be *in*consistent with justice and compassion as they are hoped for in the reign of God. That was the problem with *Deutsches Christentum,*[7] as one example.

Once we have attended to the particularities of the language we will use when we talk about God, we can begin to think about its truth.

Moreover, if the truth by which we live our lives is "Jesus is God," how does that truth reveal itself through our lives? How do we live such that our language and the authorities to whom we give our allegiance are coherent with our thinking and our actions? What does it mean to bet our lives on the assertion that "Jesus is God"? As we work toward clear understandings of what is required by language, authority, and coherence, we must ask: Are they consistent with the truthfulness of the Christian Gospel?

Truthfulness and plausibility. Attending to the truthfulness of the Christian Gospel means formulating a structure of plausibility. Now at this point we often feel uneasy, for we do not know how to connect faith and plausibility—but this reveals the influence that Immanuel Kant (1724-1804) has had on our way of knowing. It was Kant who said that the *knowings* of faith are of a lower order than the *knowings* that take place through pure understanding, or the pure operation of the intellect. In fact, Kant would say that they—that is, the *knowings* of faith—are not in a very real sense *knowings* at all.

The problem with Kant's proposal was the resulting inference that that which cannot be known or demonstrated is a matter of faith. I resist this! Moreover, I resist all language that refers to religions as "communities of faith." If you think about what we actually do with the way we live our lives, we can say that banking is a "community of faith." For example, I have invested a portion of my income every month in my church pension: That is an act of faith! Who knows whether or not I should do this? Who knows whether or not it is the best thing to do? So, in one sense, the pension operation, which functions purely with numbers and interest rates and other intellectual data, is a "community of faith"—as much of a "community of faith" as the people who gather together at a church on Sunday mornings. This means we succumb to Kant's understanding of knowing if we juxtapose or contrast plausibility with faith.

The fact is that plausibility is utterly consistent with faith, for faith in the public sense means committing oneself in life and in death to one specific vision or expectation of the future. Suppose that I say that the future means "Work, work, save, save, build a house, croak" (which is a Bavarian proverb: "*Arbeit, Arbeit, Spar, Spar, bau ein Häusele, veredce*"). To live according to this vision of the future says that life is essentially not very meaningful, and when you die, that's the end: Do we *know* that? A fair amount of evidence can be offered to make it a plausible assertion, right? But we don't *know* it with absolute certainty. Nevertheless, one could live one's whole life as if that were, in fact, true. You could spend your life trying to accumulate whatever you can, live as comfortably as you can, and when you die, kick up your heels and let them do whatever they want. That is, indeed, a way of living one's life "in faith." Well, what kind of faith? It is faith that there is *nothing* after one dies—and therefore, one could argue, not much before.

Or, it is also possible, if you will go along with this, to say, "When you die, Jupiter will send you to Hades." That's a possibility; it has less plausibility now than it did in the Roman Empire, but it is a thinkable thing. And it has less plausibility than the idea that when you die there is nothing! But it is a possibility.

Or I could say that Jesus of Nazareth is in charge of the final future, and whatever happens, I'm going to live my life as if that were the truth. Dietrich Bonhoeffer did that, as one example. In the same way, I am going to say that this alternative—Jesus of Nazareth is in charge of the final future—is as plausible as the other two. Then, when we have rooted out the options and looked at their plausibility, we will be able to say which of them—x, y, or z—one commits to, or lives one's life by, or trusts in life and death. The Christian good news is that Jesus of Nazareth has been raised from death, that death no longer has dominion over him. I have bet my living, and now I am called to bet my dying, that Jesus will have the last word.[8]

Christian theology, therefore, offers a plausible vision of the future grounded in the claim that Jesus is the crucified and risen Messiah of Israel and the world. Christian faith means entrusting oneself in life and death to Jesus as the Christ.

Judaism as Grounding for the Concept of Resurrection

Accounts of Jewish acceptance of the idea of resurrection are found in Old Testament texts written nearly 200 years before Jesus was born. Daniel 12:2 hints at resurrection when he claims that "(m)any of those who sleep in the dust of the earth shall awake." Likewise, in 2 Maccabees 7:22-23, a mother who lost seven sons because they would not accept a false god claimed that her children would not be lost forever. She clearly relied on Jewish recognition of the concept of resurrection when she said, "I do not know how you came into being in my womb. It was not I who gave you life and breath, nor I who set in order the elements within each of you. Therefore the Creator of the world, who shaped the beginning of humankind and devised the origin of all things, will in his mercy give life and breath back to you again, since you now forget yourselves for the sake of his laws."

Like other second-Temple (536 B.C. to 70 A.D.) Jews, this woman believed in resurrection. We also know that the general expectation of resurrection was connected not only to the re-embodiment of persons who already had died, but also with the inauguration of a new covenant with God in which all righteous persons would be simultaneously raised.[9]

At the opposite end of the spectrum, Romans and those particular Jews who opposed Jesus expected crucifixion to be the end of Jesus and his mission. When some observed Jesus performing signs, they told the priests, and on hearing their report, the priests called a council meeting. They worried about a Roman response to Jesus' actions. In John 11:49-50, the chief priest Caiaphas prophesied, "You know nothing at all! You do not understand that it is better for you to have one man die for the people than to have the whole nation destroyed."

Insight into how the resurrection event was understood in first-century Israel also is provided by contemporary Jewish New Testament scholar Pinchas Lapide, who says, "Resurrection, exaltation, and glorification are understood not as Jesus' own deed, but, in good Jewish manner, as a raising by God, as a gracious deed of God on the crucified Jesus."[10]

A number of New Testament texts support Lapide's claim, among them, Acts 2:22-24 and 36:[11]

> You that are Israelites, listen to what I have to say: Jesus of Nazareth, a man attested to you by God with deeds of power, wonders, and signs that God did through him among you, as you yourselves know—this man, handed over to you according to the definite plan and foreknowledge of God, you crucified and killed by the hands of those outside the law. But God raised him up, having freed him from death, because it was impossible for him to be held in its power. . . . Therefore let the entire house of Israel know with certainty that God has made him both Lord and Messiah, this Jesus whom you crucified.

God raised Jesus up. That is, God did it. Humankind proclaimed—and still proclaims—this event, and its truth is central to the witness of the earliest followers of Jesus. It made sense to the disciple community because the *idea* of resurrection was a tenet of their faith, and because the *event* of resurrection was consistent with their Jewish belief system, it also definitively meant that God was present in their midst.

The Gospels repeatedly describe God's favor with Jesus. In Matthew, Jesus is depicted as the "one who abides with his people"[12] and who is understood to be the "exalted teacher of the church."[13] Markan texts call Jesus the "one who died on the cross for sins."[14] Luke's Gospel is interested in Jesus as the "one whose words and deeds liberate those who are oppressed"[15] and says "(T)his Jesus (is) Lord and Christ."[16] The Book of John points to Jesus as the "one who reveals what God is truly like"[17] and refers to him as the "glorified Son of God."[18] Each Gospel writer presents a distinctive view of the way in which Jesus faced the ultimate crisis: whether to escape the cross in a completely understandable effort of self-preservation, or to trust that God's mission for the world would be fulfilled—indeed could only be fulfilled by submitting to death at the hands of his own people. Jesus' response to that crisis revealed not only Jesus' integrity and commitment to God, but also that Jesus' submission to death is the high point in human history.[19] Lapide provides a unique affirmation of this claim:

> I am completely convinced that the Twelve from Galilee, who were all farmers, shepherds, and fishermen—there was not a single theology professor to be found among them—were totally unimpressed by scholarly theologoumena. . . . If they, through such a concrete historical event as the crucifixion, were so totally in despair and crushed, as all the four evangelists report to us, then no less concrete a historical event was needed in order to bring them out of the deep valley of their despair and within a short time to transform them into a community of salvation rejoicing to the high heavens.[20]

The resurrection is then a high point of divine history: Humanity's clear "no" to God is returned with God's "yes" to the creation. As Günther Bornkamm points out, "(f)or the disciples . . . the appearances of the risen One and their experience of his presence in the Spirit meant that his end was a new beginning, in the sense of a final and absolute act of God for the salvation of the world. Men [sic] had condemned Jesus, but God turned their no into a yes. In that yes God committed himself [sic] irrevocably to the world that rejected him."[21]

Just so, after the event of the cross and resurrection, nothing would ever be the same.

Event as History

What does it mean to call the resurrection an event? An event is an occurrence which has taken place within time. Events happen. They are experiential. That is, sensory data help people describe the details of what transpires when an event occurs.

The raw data of an event cannot stand alone, however. For data to have meaning, it must be organized in our minds and understood within a particular framework or worldview. We must be able to interpret data in such a way that it helps us make sense of the world.[22] Here we would do well to refer to the Kantian *Critique of Pure Reason,* a rigorous analysis of how humanity can claim to have any authentic theoretical (or pure) knowledge. For Kant, "theoretical" knowledge is contrasted with "practical" knowledge—for example, in the sense that automotive engineering precedes the functioning of an automobile: The function of the automobile is practical, and the theoretical analyses that are required to make an internal combustion engine precedes any practical manufacture of such a device. Here "theoretical" is not a dream world or an unreal world. It is, in fact, the most "real," the most necessary, and that which is required prior to anything done practically.

The question then for Kant is how we can have any authentic, theoretical, or pure knowledge. In response to this question, he demonstrated that all authentic theoretical knowing involves two dimensions: 1) the organizing categories of the mind, and 2) the functioning of these categories brought to bear on the raw data mediated by the senses. What we are trying to say here is that without interpretations, bare facts do not make sense, for we do not know how to think about them. For example, if I simply announce to you that someone named Jesus was executed by the Romans in 30-or-so A.D. by our reckoning and that he was later encountered by people, then you can say, "This is crazy! It doesn't make sense!" Nonsense occurs when we have only data, but not its interpretation. To be able to claim that the Gospel means "good news"—not only "good," but also "news"—we need to know what it means and how to understand it.

Without the "news" aspect, there is nothing to tell. And without interpretation, we cannot determine whether or why the news is, in fact, good.

Judaism as Grounding for the Christian Gospel

The documents of the New Testament use a variety of literary devices to tell, interpret, and proclaim the saving, good news of Jesus' death and resurrection. The story cannot be understood authentically apart from its indispensable matrix in Israel: Israel's history, literature, worship, ethos, and expectations reveal the context from which Jesus' disciples understood the world. They also show how that context enabled them to make sense of what was going on with the event of the resurrection.

Two fundamental lenses clarified and gave meaning to the raw data of this event: an eschatological lens and an apocalyptic lens. First, the eschatological lens refers to the disciples' understanding of events as actions that take place in time. Here we must understand what we mean by "eschatological." The root word "eschaton" is Greek, and refers to an "end"—not in the sense of a conclusion, but in the sense of an outcome. For example, marriage is the eschatological outcome of courtship. After a couple is married, we can look back at their first meeting, the unfolding and developing of their relationship together, and their commitment to one another—but it is the marriage, the *outcome*, which calls our attention to the process. If they go their separate ways, even remaining friends, the outcome does not claim the same level of importance.

Hence, to say that the disciples' understanding of events occurring in time was eschatological is to say that they expected events to be understood only from the end of history, so that looking back at them one might validate the claims these events make on truth. Outcome reveals the *meaning* of events. Since the disciples realized that God is active in the unfolding of events in the world, they understood that God's activity as revealed in history is directed toward a meaningful outcome in the future.

Secondly, the disciples assumed an apocalyptic understanding of history. The word "apocalyptic" refers to a dramatic divine intervention in an otherwise hopeless situation.[23] To say that the disciples understood history to be apocalyptic is to ground the notion that they believed that God could intervene in tragic and shameful events by vindicating a martyr, and that this intervention could occur through resuscitation or through eschatological resurrection.

To summarize these two lenses, then, the disciples believed that God was active in the events of the world. They also were open to an apocalyptic intervention in world events. Because this is the framework from which they viewed the world in which they lived, they experienced what happened to Jesus as eschatological resurrection—as God's intervention in a hopeless situation such that the outcome of history is revealed.

Christians also claim that the resurrection of Jesus is true. It was an event that occurred in the history of the world. This claim forms the basis for asserting the good news that Jesus is, indeed, the Messiah, and that as such he is beyond death and its power. The character of this claim is that Jesus' resurrection grounds the Christian worldview. Jesus' resurrection encounters us. It alters us. And in so doing, it informs how we understand other happenings or events—for we see them through the eyes of the One who has been resurrected and through whom we understand God's yes for the world.

The Resurrection as Historical Event

The various New Testament accounts of the resurrection appearances of Jesus cannot be harmonized so as to remove the numerous discrepancies that appear in these texts. However, these discrepancies support the presumption that the various traditions arose independently.[24]

A number of factors come together to show the disciples' awareness of God's hand in the post-resurrection accounts of Jesus: a) the tomb was empty; b) women were reported to be among the earliest witnesses of the empty tomb; and c) the disciples were encountered by appearances of Jesus.[25]

Reports of the empty tomb do not stand alone. First, no interest was shown in either the tomb itself or in Jesus' artifacts. Atypically, no devotions or prayers on Jesus' behalf were offered at the tomb. Also, some scholars wonder why there was never any question of the second burial rite which should have been performed for Jesus, had he died and not been resurrected. Following first-century burial customs, a dead person was laid in a grave until the flesh was gone and only the bones remained. Then the bones were buried so that on the last day, God could call up all the people who already died and resurrect them. The fact that this did not happen with Jesus points to the community's awareness of his resurrection and the transformation of his body.[26]

Secondly, all four Gospels attribute the empty tomb discovery to women. Now, this may not seem to be an unusual course of events today, but in the first century, a woman's status and witness were not as highly regarded as those of a man. If Gospel writers wanted to make up a story about the empty tomb, they would not have suggested that its discovery originated with women. This means the best explanation we have for the consistency of the Gospels on this subject is that all four of the authors must have remembered the discovery of the empty tomb as it actually occurred: The witnesses were women.

Thirdly, as to Jesus' appearances, numerous texts report that he was seen alive after his crucifixion, and the variety of sources asserting these occurrences also is good reason for trusting the resurrection story. Jesus was seen at the tomb, in Galilee, and along the road. He ate with the disciples. He showed them his wounds. He was recognizable. These episodes point to a certain continuity between the One who was crucified and the One who encountered the disciples after his execution.

Also notice that the detail surrounding the disciples' experiences of the risen Christ is rich in its realism. Jesus appeared and then disappeared. He was finally acknowledged after initially not being recognized by his own disciples. He was bodily present, and yet he was transformed. No allusion is made to blinding light or dazzling glory or seeing Jesus wreathed in clouds—any of which would have been a use of language typical of the Jewish apocalyptic or mystical traditions, says N. T. Wright. "The portrait of Jesus himself in these stories does not appear to have been modeled on existing stories of 'supernatural appearances.' It was not created out of expectation alone."[27] On the contrary, it is both plausible and reasonable to believe their experiences were reported as they occurred.

In describing Jesus' appearances, Wright says, "Paul provides the underlying theoretical framework: an event for which there was no precedent and of which there remains as yet no subsequent example, an event involving neither the resuscitation nor the abandonment of a physical body, but its transformation to a new form of physicality."[28]

Wright says that the empty tomb reports and the many encounters with the risen Jesus are enough to convince him of the truthfulness of Jesus' resurrection. He says the early Christians

> . . . did not invent the empty tomb and the "meetings" or "sightings" of the risen Jesus in order to explain a faith they already had. They developed that faith because of the occurrence, and the convergence, of these two phenomena. Nobody was expecting this kind of thing; no kind of conversion-experience would have generated such ideas; nobody would have invented it, no matter how guilty (or how forgiven) they felt, no matter how many hours they pored over the scriptures. To suggest otherwise is to stop doing history and to enter into a fantasy world. . . .[29]

Wright is saying that, from his perspective, the empty tomb and the appearances of the risen Jesus are enough "evidence" to conclude that the resurrection reports are accurate.

Following reports of Jesus' resurrection, the disciples attributed him both in language and in practice with divine references. They engaged in acts of veneration and worship toward him. Salvation was preached "in Jesus' name."[30] Signs were done "in Jesus' name."[31] Prayers were addressed to Jesus.[32] Hymns were sung about Jesus[33] and to Jesus.[34] And persons were baptized into the name of Jesus.[35]

To this collection of post-resurrection messianic references, James D. G. Dunn offers another point. He refers to Matthew 28:17 as a strong indication that reports of the disciples' experiences with Jesus were genuine, for "When they saw him, they worshiped him, but some doubted."[36] The inclusion of the point that some doubted contains a ring of truth, says Dunn. Again, the author of Matthew would have written this testimony only if it were true. The fact that there is no later mention that the doubts of these persons were resolved also lends credence to the authenticity of the text.[37] That is, they were not written merely to show that everyone supported the author's point of view. Matthew took a risk by acknowledging that even some disciples remained unconvinced.

Furthermore, the occasion to "doubt" does not precede a decision but follows it. For example, if people wonder about the rightness of a position, their doubt comes about after they obligate themselves one way or another. Obligation or commitment can be seen in the Matthean text, above, in the form of worship. The people obligate themselves in their worship of the resurrected Jesus. And some of them also doubt. In this way, doubt is not the absence of faith, but faith's constant companion.

Coming to Terms with the Resurrection of Jesus

"In the New Testament there is no faith that does not start *a priori* with the resurrection of Jesus," says Jürgen Moltmann. "A Christian faith that is not resurrection faith can therefore be called neither Christian nor faith."[38]

Noting that the resurrection identifies Jesus as the Messiah of Israel and the eschatological Lord of history, he adds that these factors are also the reasons why Christians pay attention to Jesus. "Christianity stands or falls with the reality of the raising of Jesus from the dead by God."[39]

Making sense of the resurrection of Jesus did not happen overnight—or over a weekend. It is more likely that coming to terms with the resurrection took place eventually—as the fullness of its implications began to reveal itself to the disciples and to those who became the church.

Events do not always seem significant at the moment of their occurring. If we don't consider them worthy of attention when they occur, we don't give them their "due." But when they happen *to* us—that is, when we are affected by them or when we allow them to inform how we think or perhaps even alter how we understand the world—then their meaning is revealed. One example is the change in attitudes toward women over the millennia. The feminist movement is only now awakening Western society to the realization that diminishing the value of some of its people reduces the worthiness even of those who are in power positions. When this realization "clicks" in the minds of people who may have held women in low regard, then—suddenly!—the meaning of the feminist movement *happens* to them. Likewise, with the civil rights movement: It *occurs* when it finally has an impact on a person. And in that instant, it is news.

News attains its legitimacy or power not at a *singular* point in time, but in a *particular* point in time. That is, events happen or become news when the realization of their meaning finally hits home. Sometimes this realization unfolds slowly, so that our knowledge is partial. Incremental "aha!" moments along the way to broader insights may come to mind— and these moments inspire the ongoing pursuit of the fullness of the truth that is to come. The fullness of the truth we anticipate will be known in its outcome. Along the way, as we seek the unveiling of God's truth, we experience its happening-to-us as news.

The Christian Gospel was good news not only in the first century. It also is good news today. And from the perspective of the Christian church, three points need to be made stemming from the good news that Jesus is risen: 1) Jesus is Lord; 2) God's plan includes the entirety of creation, and that plan is redemption; and 3) our understanding of the past must be re-interpreted in light of the revelation of God's plan to redeem the creation.

Jesus is Lord. In the introduction of his letter to the Romans,[40] the apostle Paul uses the messianic title Son of God when referring to Jesus. He says that the Gospel he wants to share is that Jesus is the Son of God made known by his resurrection from the dead.

We often refer to Paul's understanding of the Gospels as justification by faith[41] or as a theology of the cross.[42] In and of themselves, both of these assertions are true, but they are consequences of the good news, not the Gospels themselves. The good news itself is, and only is, that Jesus is risen and Jesus is the Messiah. All other claims are based on the truth of this Gospel.

The truth that Jesus of Nazareth was resurrected to a new sort of life is also the best explanation for the rise of the early church. The disciples did not conceive of the resurrection as "a messy accident, the end of a beautiful dream, but rather the climactic saving act of the God of Israel, the one God of all the earth; and why, in consequence, they, to their own astonishment, arrived at the conclusion that Jesus of Nazareth had done what, according to the Scriptures, only Israel's God could do."[43]

As the reality of their experience with Jesus' resurrection set in, the central tenets of their faith were strengthened so that they became a messianic movement within Israel. Wright explains their understanding of the resurrection thusly:

> This was what made them not only speak of the one true God, but invoke him, pray to him, love him and serve him in terms of the Father and the lord, of the God who sent the Son and now sends the Spirit of the Son, in terms of the only-begotten God who makes visible the otherwise invisible creator of the world. This is why, when they spoke of the resurrection of Jesus, they spoke of the resurrection of the Son of God.[44]

Just so, when Paul greets the Romans in his letter, he offers grace and peace "from God our Father and the Lord Jesus Christ."

God's plan for the entire creation is redemption. In the context of the Christian ethic, it is important here to assert that, in contrast to the Greeks, Jews and Christians affirmed the world as creation and God as creator. The world is not "emanation," something that can happen without volition. Hence, "creation" means more than that the world can be differentiated from God. To say that the world is "creation" means that it is intended by God, wanted by God, willed into existence by God. Finally, the Christian doctrine of creation, because it is world-affirming, means that Christians are called necessarily to stewardship, not exploitation, of the world. We make the point here, then, that God's plan for the entire creation is *redemption*—and that God's redemption plan is for the *entire creation*.

Redemption is promised through Jesus' resurrection. The meaning of Jesus' resurrection includes the recognition that the eschatological messianic age has come, that Jesus is the eschatological Messiah, and that he has the power of the future. This future transcends time and space, even as it is taking place in time and space.

Wright tells us that "there is virtually no evidence that Jews were expecting the end of the space-time universe."[45] They did not anticipate a catastrophic end of all of creation, such as, for example, Stephen Hawking's "big crunch."[46] Nor did they seek a heavenly place—a repository where souls reside after death. Neither did they imagine, at the fiction end of the spectrum, the arrival of space ships to collect truly God-fearing Christians and rescue them to some far-off safe haven, with everyone else "left behind" to perish with the destruction of God's creation. Such notions never occurred to them; indeed, they are the result of scientific speculation or human fiction.

As we should expect, Jesus' teachings about the future reflect Jewish thinking. He proclaimed the rule of God as "a reality belonging to the future. This is the coming kingdom. The idea was not new, being a conventional aspect of Jewish expectation," says Pannenberg. "What was new was Jesus' understanding that God's claim on the world is to be viewed exclusively in terms of his coming rule."[47]

1 Corinthians 15: 20-28 provides insight into how Jesus' resurrection shaped the early Christians' understanding of this power of the future:

> But in fact Christ has been raised from the dead, the first fruits of those who have died. For since death came through a human being, the resurrection of the dead has also come through a human being; for as all die in Adam, so all will be made alive in Christ. But each in his own order: Christ the first fruits, then at his coming those who belong to Christ. Then comes the end, when he hands over the kingdom to God the Father, after he has destroyed every ruler and every authority and power. For he must reign until he has put all his enemies under his feet. The last enemy to be destroyed

is death. For "God has put all things in subjection under his feet." But when it says, "All things are put in subjection," it is plain that this does not include the one who put all things in subjection under him. When all things are subjected to him, then the son himself will also be subjected to the one who put all things in subjection under him, so that God may be all in all.

If the last enemy to be destroyed is death, and the Risen Jesus is the power of the future, then God's plan for the creation is redemption. In the resurrection appearances, the disciples encountered the parousia (that is, the "coming" and "presence" of the Messiah as the outcome of history) in the midst of history. To say it another way, they experienced the resurrection as a proleptic event, a preview of the outcome of history in the midst of their own time and place—and as such, they encountered Jesus as the Messiah, for "he is the one ordained by God as the judge of the living and the dead."[48]

Today, life lived in acceptance of God's promise to redeem the creation is like reading a mystery book in which we are offered a look at God's last chapter. We know the outcome, but do not know the plot. However, knowing the outcome changes radically the way we participate in the plot!

Said another way, God's agenda is life, not death. If death were God's intended outcome, Jesus would have stayed dead. However, we Christians bet our lives on our belief that God's promise, revealed in the risen Jesus, is to redeem the creation.

Re-appropriate the past. To re-appropriate is to retake possession of—and here, it is to reclaim an idea, and to do so with authority. The resurrection of Jesus authorized—indeed, required—the disciple community to re-appropriate both the experience of Jesus and the history of Israel. That's what they are doing in the Gospels.

Even today we do not begin to give attention to persons in history from their beginnings, but from some later point in their lives. For example, nobody sat around in Plains, Georgia, on the day of Jimmy Carter's birth and said, "The fortieth president of the U.S. was born this morning to his mother, etc." It doesn't work that way! Later, when Carter became president, we went to look at Plains. So it's only at the end—or at some other point later—that we begin to pay attention. And to this we can say that the claims of and about Jesus receive attention only from the *outcome* of his history. Hence, the resurrection of Jesus is decisive for both the fact and the form of the Gospel tradition.

Since there is ample evidence to validate Jesus' crucifixion and resurrection, these events must be considered with regard to their meaning for all of creation. The disciples were the first to take on this responsibility. The truth they experienced awakened them to a new worldview—one which they had accepted as a part of their Jewish beliefs, but had not grasped fully. When they finally took God's essential message of forgiveness and the redemption of the creation into their faith as something that was real and true, they understood the same historical events and texts differently. Passages they knew well enough to repeat word-for-word suddenly had new and deeper meanings.

The role of the God of Israel as both its final judge and the judge of all creation was well established in Jewish history. In light of Jesus' teachings, death, and resurrection, the disciples now placed the risen Christ in that same uniquely divine role. The resurrection appearances let the disciples discern a shocking outcome: The judgment has already happened. Ultimately, they understood that God forgives Israel, and that Israel's history points to the climactic moment in which Jesus is risen. And because they not only know the identity of the judge, they then also know the verdict—and it is Yes! Paul's letter to the Corinthians coincides with the way they re-envision history when he says, "As surely as God is faithful, our word to you has not been 'Yes and No.' For the Son of God, Jesus Christ, whom we proclaimed among you, Silvanus and Timothy and I, was not 'Yes and No'; but in him, it is always 'Yes.'"[49]

The reason we can claim that the Gospel is news is because God did something radical in the resurrection of Jesus. The resurrection had meaning for the people of Israel; it continues to have meaning for us today, for in this event, God reveals a promise that continues to unfold in our midst. This is the essential nature of divine promise: it is given . . . and we await its fulfillment. This is *news*!

HOSEA 11: 8-9

How can I give you up, Ephraim?

How can I hand you over, O Israel?

How can I make you like Admah?

How can I treat you like Zeboiim?

My heart recoils within me;

my compassion grows warm and tender.

I will not execute my fierce anger;

I will not again destroy Ephraim;

for I am God and no mortal,

the Holy One in your midst,

and I will not come in wrath.

CHAPTER 2

THE CONFESSION THAT JESUS IS GOD

"Christ" is the Greek translation of the Jewish title "Messiah," and so christology begins by acknowledging that Jesus is the Christ.[50] My whole attempt to explicate christology begins immediately with the church's final confession, "Jesus of Nazareth is God." In a sense what we're doing from the resurrection is both re-anticipating the future and re-appropriating the past—so I'm moving in two directions out of the resurrection.

To declare this truth as dramatically as possible, we again say that Jesus of Nazareth, born of Mary and executed under Pontius Pilate, Roman procurator of Judea from 26 to 36 A.D., is God.

Jesus is God.

The task. Chapter 1 paid attention to the good news of the resurrection of Jesus as an event which occurred in history and as grounding for the early church. The basic teaching of the church is "christology": thought and words confessing Jesus of Nazareth as the Messiah of Israel. Jesus is the Messiah, the Christ, and it is this conviction which makes one a Christian. The task of Chapter 2 is to show how the good news, which inspired the proclamation and teaching of the church, led to and requires the truth of the claim that Jesus of Nazareth is God.

An understanding of the material in this chapter is essential, for it will establish a structure upon which we will build arguments in the rest of the book. Here we will need to say many things at the same time, because when they are considered together, important connections can be made. Some points probably will be new to you; others will be correctives to common but unsupportable assumptions, or clarifications that need to be asserted. In the end, our task is to show beyond question that the resurrection of Jesus could mean only one thing to the disciples—and that it can mean only one thing today. Moreover, the church is based on that truth: Jesus is God.

Jewish Worldview Points to Confession of Jesus as Divine

The christological approach advocated in this task can be described as a historical method which ascertains how Jesus' disciples moved from knowledge of his resurrection to the confession that Jesus is God. What was it about their worldview that pointed them to such an admission?

With these insights, we can investigate what the term "God" means when it is understood historically and eschatologically—that is, in terms of the future, or in terms of concepts such as "ultimacy" and "finality."

To intelligently consider these points, we need criteria by which we can determine what we mean when we assert that something or someone is divine. We also need standards for determining whether or not a claim is truthful. Finally, we must define what is meant by the term "faith."

Basis for christology. Christology is the study of Jesus, the crucified and risen Messiah of Israel. Carl Braaten provides a cautious definition that can help us get started:

> Christology is the interpretation of Jesus of Nazareth as the Christ of God from the standpoint of the faith of the Christian church. The word "christology" means literally the *logos* about *Christos*, thought and speech about Christ. Christ is a title, and not the second name of Jesus. The title expresses the identity of Jesus of Nazareth, according to the apostolic witness and the catholic tradition.[51]

The fundamental question which we must address here is "why do we pay attention to Jesus?" Similarly, Pannenberg asked, "What are we doing with this Jew?" To that, someone might add, "Why not Thor?" Or why not some other ancestral deities? So again, we return to the fundamental question: Why Jesus?

To get at this question, we need to know what it means to confess that Jesus is the "Christ." Moltmann makes a similar point:

> For a long time one of the important questions in modern christology was the transition from "the Jesus of History" to "the Christ of faith." . . . I have come to find another question more important still, because it is more "down to earth"—more "embodied." This question is the path leading from the Jewish Jesus to the Christian Jesus, and the rediscovery of the Jewish Jesus in the Christian Jesus.[52]

We must recover the basis for the claim in the disciples' realization that Jesus is the crucified and risen Messiah of Israel. Out of this understanding we can explore the basis for the claim that Jesus is God.

We all know the passion story in which Jesus was crucified and resurrected. In the midst of this narrative—as it was happening to the disciples—they moved from knowledge about the event of Jesus' resurrection to the realization and confession that Jesus is God.

The question we must ask is what it was about their worldview that pointed them to this admission. Why did their proclamation regarding the divinity of Jesus not violate their Jewish belief in Yahweh?

The Jewish concept of God. In Israel, God is identified by historical events which are recorded, for example, in Exodus 20:2, which says, "I am the Lord your God, who brought you out of the land of Egypt, out of the house of slavery."

For Jews, the identity of "God" arising out of these events refers to the electing God—that is, the God who elects, or chooses, the people of Israel. It also refers to the compassionate God—that is, the God who is present to Israel, who rescues and accompanies the people; and finally, it is the vulnerable God, who cannot leave Israel to its own devices, but must provide the law and lead with God's Spirit. Exodus 6:2-8 is one witness among many in the unfolding story of God with the people of Israel:

> God also spoke to Moses and said to him: "I am the Lord.
> I appeared to Abraham, Isaac and Jacob as God Almighty,

but by my name, 'The Lord,' I did not make myself known to them. I also established my covenant with them, to give them the land of Canaan, the land in which they resided as aliens. I have also heard the groaning of the Israelites whom the Egyptians are holding as slaves, and I have remembered my covenant. Say therefore to the Israelites, "I am the Lord, and I will free you from the burdens of the Egyptians and deliver you from slavery to them. I will redeem you with an outstretched arm and with mighty acts of judgment. I will take you as my people, and I will be your God. You shall know that I am the Lord your God, who has freed you from the burdens of the Egyptians. I will bring you into the land that I swore to give to Abraham, Isaac and Jacob; I will give it to you for a possession. I am the Lord."

The people of Israel relied on the Exodus narrative to differentiate God from deities venerated by surrounding nations. They also relied on this story of their experiences with God to understand God and to inform their prayers that God would continue to be with them. As Wright explains, "Part of the story was precisely the discovery of what God's faithfulness and rescuing power would look like in practice—or to put it another way, what the strange name of God, YHWH, might actually mean."[53]

The writings of the second-Temple period (536 B.C. to 70 A.D.)[54] reveal additional features of Jewish writings with regard to first-century Israel's understanding of God. First, since they believed that God had abandoned Jerusalem at the time of the exile, they looked for YHWH[55] to return. And secondly, they sought a Messiah—that is, a surprising political hope. By this we mean that they expected some sort of fulfillment of the enthronement of YHWH.[56] They remembered 2 Samuel 7 (Nathan's prophecy), which told the Jews of God's plan to establish a kingdom out of the house of David. Likewise, Psalm 2 (the royal coronation hymn) describes "Messiah" as one of the titles for the king of Israel—a title which evolved to represent the name for the ideal king of the hoped-for restoration, one who would once again lead the people out of exile.

Wright reminds us that "when YHWH acted in history, the agent through whom he acted would be vindicated, exalted, and honored in a quite unprecedented manner."[57] The key point here is that these ideas of who-God-was were plausible from a Jewish perspective. The concepts were neither self-contradictory nor a threat to Israel's understanding of monotheism.[58] Rather, says Wright, "(t)hey were attempts to find out what that monotheism actually meant in practice. . . . Jewish monotheism was much more complicated than was supposed by those who said so glibly that since Jews were monotheists they could not conceive of a human being as divine."[59]

Indeed, for many people, the disciples among them, such ideas were absolutely thinkable.

Resurrection: from vindication to announcement. Today we know Jesus' resurrection as a historical truth which is the grounding, or basis, of Christianity. We know this event as something which happened at a particular time and in a particular place, and we accept this truth as the story of our faith. Indeed, we worship Jesus as the Son within the Triune God.

Many of us were born into families who already had accepted this faith, or we came to our faith by what we perceived to be Christian leanings within our culture. The disciples, on the other hand, received neither of these influences—neither family nor culture—so we have to ask: How did they come to understand that Jesus—who had been arrested and crucified for crimes against the Roman empire—was the Son of God?

Wright says the answer comes by understanding that "Jesus had been executed as a messianic pretender, as 'king of the Jews,' and Israel's (G)od had vindicated him." That is, in the resurrection, God was fulfilling the promises God had made to the people of Israel—and more: *God was revealing God to be God*. As Wright explains, then, "They saw the resurrection as a life-giving act of the covenant God, the Creator who had always had the power to kill and make alive, who indeed was different from the other gods precisely in this respect."[60]

The disciples also remembered texts describing the one they hoped would redeem the people of Israel from their enemies. The royal coronation hymn (Psalm 2: 7b-8—"You are my son; today I have begotten you. Ask of me, and I will make the nations your heritage, and the ends of the earth your possession.") reveals God's willingness to deliver all of creation to God's begotten Son. In this way, says Wright, "The resurrection means that Jesus is the messianic 'Son of God'; that Israel's eschatological hope has been fulfilled; that it is time for the nations of the world to be brought into submission to Israel's god."[61]

Wright adds that Jesus is the Son of God not only in the sense that he is the Messiah, but more: He is "the one in whom the living God, Israel's God, has become personally present in the world." In this he insists that Jesus did not "become" the Son of God through the resurrection, but rather, that *both* his ministry *and* his death-and-resurrection are to be understood as the actions of God's Son, *"and that the resurrection declared that this had been the case."*[62] That is, Jesus did not *become* the Son of God through the resurrection; rather, the resurrection was the means by which it was *announced* that Jesus was and always had been the Son of God.

The "last word" reveals what it means to be "divine." To be recognized as being "divine"—that is, to be recognized as God—we must first define who or what the term "God" means. In a Jewish context, "God" means whoever or whatever brings deliverance. When this is translated into an eschatological view of history, God can be understood as either our *highest value* (specifically, what we value most above all else) or as that which has the *last word.* And Jesus qualifies on both grounds.

First, we must recall how the disciples dedicated their lives to the proclamation of Jesus and, indeed, gave up their lives for the sake of the truth of their proclamation: They would not deny Jesus. Jesus was their highest value.

Jesus was proclaimed as being in some sense "vindicated." However, his resurrection was fundamentally not a victory for himself, but rather, on behalf of others. We recall that Paul said that by the Messiah's suffering, Jesus was the first to rise from the dead (1 Corinthians 15:20). In fact, Christ has been raised from the dead, the first fruits of those who have died, and that, according to Acts 26:23, "he would proclaim light both to our people and to the Gentiles."[63]

Moreover, Jesus' followers proclaimed his resurrection not only for Israel, but ultimately for all (1 Corinthians 15:20-23). "All" meant everyone—not a narrow national triumph, such as the restoration of Israel's sovereignty, or the return to Davidic greatness and Solomonic splendor. Rather, they announced the final grounding of Israel's universal calling for the sake of all nations, "a light for revelation to the Gentiles and for glory to your people Israel" (Luke 2:32).[64]

Through Jesus, then, God's eschatological salvation is completed. And here we can say that Jesus is the "alpha" and the "omega," the One whose resurrection signals the beginning of the redemption of the world, and whose future signals its completion.

Secondly, identifying the One who has the last word identifies God. Here we can say that Jesus has the last word. As we discussed in chapter 1, "he is the one ordained by God as the judge of the living and the dead."[65] To be clear, Jesus who died on a cross and was resurrected by God so that God's love for the creation might be revealed now claims the creation, and stands on its behalf. He alone determines its worthiness. He alone is its judge.

Furthermore, to say that Jesus is God means to believe that he is the author and the consummator of the final saving outcome. That is, as author, he writes the final chapter, and as consummator, he brings about the promised redemption of the creation.

The Messiah's mission has to do with the future, but it is a future which transcends time and space, even as it is taking place in time and space. The full meaning of the resurrection of Jesus includes the recognition that the eschatological messianic age has come. Jesus is the eschatological Messiah in that he has the power of the future. Christians now live their lives according to that announcement.

"The idea of power makes sense only in relation to a future," says Pannenberg. "Only he who has a future is in possession of power."[66] So Jesus, the One who has the last word, is God.

The Confession of Jesus' Divinity to Non-Jews

The Jewish recognition of Jesus' divinity requires a Jewish understanding of God. From the perspective of the disciples, Jesus alone has the power of the future, for he alone has been raised from the dead. As Paul points out in Romans 6:9, "death no longer has dominion over him."

Furthermore, as the One who has the power of the future, only Jesus can make unconditional promises. His activity and proclamation point to promises inherent in the redemptive reign of God. That is, Jesus not only professed to represent God's reign; he also taught with authority and acted with sovereign freedom in his relationships with "sinners" and Gentiles.[67] At stake in these actions was not an announcement of some sort of supernatural divinity; rather, they were Jesus' claim to embody and enact eschatological and messianic deliverance and salvation. That is, all of Jesus' actions pointed to and initiated God's final outcome of redemption for the creation. Ultimately, this is the good news that the disciples wanted to share with the world.

But how? As shown at the beginning of this chapter, the meaning of the term "god" is not necessarily self-evident. What happens when the Jewish confession of Jesus' divinity is integrated into the Hellenistic world?

A Greek interpretation of the term "god." Among the Greeks, the meaning of "god" focused on attributes of a deity: A "god" was said to be infinite, immortal, impassible, and unmoved or untouched by the world; in a word, supernatural.[68] To be supernatural means to be "attributed to or thought to reveal some force above the laws of nature."[69] That is, the Hellenistic idea of god had nothing to do with that which was material, concrete, or sensory. (Recall that the Jewish understanding of god is based on the One who is revealed in history—through events which occur in a particular place and at a particular time, and are, therefore, material, concrete, and sensory.) As Robert Jenson points out, the reason the Greeks thought of "god" in these terms is because they understood involvement in the natural world to be corrupting, destructive, and subject to the ravages of decay and decline and, finally, death.[70] To protect "god" from that kind of ravaging, their approach understood "god" to be supernatural—that is, beyond or outside nature altogether, and untouched by anything, whether historical or sensual.[71]

Furthermore, the Greeks thought the world was an emanation[72] and, in its highest form, was immaterial. They claimed that the world's existence had nothing to do with a "god" willing it or wanting it. They said the world was not an intention—and this approach is quite different from calling the world a "creation." Indeed, from the Jewish perspective, the creation *is* intended, wanted and willed—by God! Therefore, when we think about the concept of "god" and the meaning of "god," we need to accentuate that the Jewish understanding of God, with God's continuous involvement in history, is quite different from the Greek understanding. The Greek idea of "god" as that which is infinite, immortal, impassible, and unmoved by the creation makes sense only if the creation itself is unimportant to the "god," only if the "god" neither deliberately brought it into being nor desired a relationship with it.

Here we see that the Greek interpretation of "god" was understood *not* from promise-and-fulfillment events in history, but from abstract concepts. What is more, the apostles who wanted to share the good news of Jesus were faced with a great many Greek misconceptions regarding the very meaning of the term "god." To apply Greek misconceptions to Jesus, the crucified messianic claimant, would have been, at best, paradoxical—for how could one who died on a cross be called impassible (that is, incapable of suffering) or untouched by the world? At the worst, such claims would be meaningless—for to maintain that someone who died is immortal would be, from a Greek perspective, absolutely absurd.

As they considered how they might proclaim the lordship of Jesus, the disciples must have realized the quandary of making sense of Jewish concepts in a Gentile world. They realized that to confess that Jesus is the author and consummator of God's eschatological salvation could *not* mean that Jesus is at the same time, illogically or miraculously, a *supernaturalistically* divine being. Divine, yes: Jesus is God. Supernatural, no: Since Jesus existed in the midst of the normal experience or knowledge of humankind, he was in "nature," and he could therefore *not* be considered supernatural.

However, the disciples could say that Jesus' lordship was qualitatively different from all other kinds of lordship. His was the lordship of life, not the lordship of death; he was the lordship of the power of the future, not of brute power over other nations. Certainly they were reminded of this by the message he shared when they were going up to Jerusalem together: "You know that among the Gentiles those whom they recognize as their rulers lord it over them, and their great ones are tyrants over them. But it is not so among you; but whoever wishes to become great among you must be your servant, and whoever wishes to be first among you must be slave of all. For the Son of Man came not to be served but to serve, and to give his life a ransom for many" (Mark 10:42-45).

Jesus is the history of something happening in God: God taking on the form of a slave and God taking on the death of a slave. In this happening, Jesus was and is the final expression of the whole Jewish experience of God. He defined the final meaning of God's electing and saving faithfulness: Death has no power.

The question for the disciples was how to explain their experiences of God through Jesus to a people whose idea of "god" was limited to that which was beyond or outside sensory material, earthly knowledge, to people whose concept of god pointed to a deity that was unfeeling and unresponsive. With such a dichotomy in worldviews, was dialogue possible? What analogies might they be able to offer?

The Logos as a starting point. The challenge for Jesus' followers was to identify concepts of "god" that could be proclaimed truthfully from a Jewish point of view, and which also would provide a basis for further discussion with non-Jews. A starting point may have been consideration of one of the various messianic titles ascribed to Jesus: "son of man." This phrase is often credited to Jesus as a self-designation in the synoptic Gospels (Matthew, Mark, and Luke), and it is likely that it referred to someone involved in eschatological judgment, as in Daniel 7:13:

> I saw one like a son of man coming with the clouds of heaven.
> And he came to the Ancient One and was presented before
> him. To him was given dominion and glory and kingship
> that all peoples, nations, and languages should serve him.

His dominion is an everlasting dominion that shall not pass away, and his kingship is one that shall never be destroyed.

The "son of man" title might be used as a synonym for the Greek concept of the divine Logos, which in Hellenism was thought to be the first emanation from God—the manifestation of rationality or meaning in the universe, or to say it another way, the first and highest intermediary creature between God and the world.[73] The *Logos* was not thought to be God, but rather, the closest being to God. Therefore, to make sense in a culture so unlike their own, the confession of Jesus as the *Logos* may have translated more intelligibly than to say that Jesus was the Messiah.

Unfortunately, other ideas previously associated with the Greek concept of the *Logos* also were ascribed to Jesus over time—and a short overview of the major arguments here is instructive. Keep in mind here that none of them ought to prevail.

First, the school of Alexandria, where Clement (150-215 A.D.) and Origen (185-254 A.D.) were scholars, taught an eternal begetting of the *Logos* from the Father: that is, they argued that the Father originated the *Logos* from the beginning of time. However, this idea also incorrectly suggested a subordination of the *Logos*.

Just 100 years later, Arius (excommunicated in 319 A.D., died ca. 335 A.D.) tried to develop ideas about how to describe Jesus as the Logos. His concern was to preserve the idea of a Greek interpretation of God: infinite, immortal, impassible and unmoved or untouched by the world—and according to these characteristics, "perfect". To accomplish his argument, Arius emphasized the Alexandrian suggestion that the *Logos* must be subordinate to God. At the same time, he proposed that God needs a mediator between God and the created world. He said that mediator is the *Logos*—who is close to God, but not quite God. In this way, the *Logos* could get stuck with being contaminated with the world of time and space—which allows for crucifixion. The separation of the *Logos* from God also assures that God is perfect.

Just six years after Arius' excommunication, the Council of Nicaea I met, and under the direction of Athanasias (296-373 A.D.), confessed that the *Logos*, understood to be the Second Person of the Holy Trinity, the Son, was fully God. The Council then wrote what has come to be known as the Nicene Creed:

> We believe in one Lord, Jesus Christ, the only Son of God, eternally begotten of the Father, God from God, Light from Light, true God from true God, *begotten, not made*, of one Being[74] with the Father. Through him all things were made.[75]

But controversies broke out after the Council of Nicaea I. Church fathers could not relate the long-held hellenistically defined characteristics of God—that is, the idea that God's perfection required that God be infinite, and so on—with the human Jesus. For one, Apollinarius of Laodicea (310-390 A.D.), who was a friend of Athanasias, taught that the *Logos* replaced the human mind of Jesus. This was a typical Greek solution: It says Jesus would have an infinite mind in a finite body; a deathless mind that will live forever, a mind which is above and beyond suffering. And it is heretical!

Another idea was put forth by Nestorius of Constantinople (381-451 A.D.), who seemed to teach that the union of the *Logos* with Jesus produced a third being: the Christ.

Finally, in 451 A.D., the Council of Chalcedon met to address the challenges arising out of the various divergent teachings. They claimed that

> (t)he Son of God and our Lord Jesus Christ is to be confessed as one and the same Person, that He is perfect in Godhead and perfect in manhood. . . . This one and the same Jesus Christ, the only begotten Son of God must be confessed to be in two natures, *not confused* and *not changed, not divided* and *not separated,* and that without the distinction of natures being taken away by such union, but rather the peculiar property of each nature being preserved and being united in one Person. . . .

The point was that if the *Logos*, understood to be the Second Person of the Holy Trinity, did not *also* assume or take on the entire human nature, then humanity could not be redeemed—for whatever is not assumed is not redeemed.[76] However, the form and content of the confession adopted at Chalcedon was ontological. Ontology refers to "beingness," so the Council members came to an agreement in defining the "beingness" of the *Logos*. Quite simply, they confessed the *Logos* as the union of two distinct and ontologically incompatible (that is, mutually exclusive) natures in one person (that is, personality)—and it was an ontological contradiction! A mortal immortal, passible impassible being? The idea was and is simply not thinkable!

Furthermore, the Chalcedon dogma recognized the *problem* instead of the *resolution*. The Council's purpose was worthy enough: Members wanted to make claims which were soteriological—that is, for the sake of belief in God's eschatological salvation: belief that God loves all of the creation and intends to carry out its redemption. However, the problem remained. If a *Logos* defined as the union of mutually exclusive beings did nothing to redeem the natural world (soteriology), then what good news was there to share (evangelism) with that world? Moreover, the only way an ontologically meaningless dogma could be held to be true is if it could be upheld by authority—and so, that's what the church did. As a result, dogma came to be accepted on the basis of papal, conciliar authority or biblical authority.

Overcoming the consequences of the dogma. The reason why assumptions about God failed at the Councils of Nicaea I and Chalcedon is simply that they directed their attention to the question of ontology: that is, they focused on the idea that supernatural beingness is the opposite of natural beingness, instead of looking to historical, relational and eschatological knowledge about God. The claims they made about God—for example, that God is impassible—did not grow out of the Jewish matrix. The history of Israel was ignored. The conclusion to be drawn is that the approach taken by the Council of Chalcedon was unhistorical, and therefore, in a real sense, also unbiblical.

Through the ages, the tendency toward acceptance of nonsensical dogma led to the notion that so-called "faith" in Christ required a sacrifice of intellect. Followers adhered to obedient confessions of a non-sensory (and therefore, nonsensical) dogma demanded by an authority—sometimes cloaked as a council, other times as a pope, or an emperor, or even a book: the Bible. Wherever these authorities have broken down, dogma has had to be abandoned.[77]

The essentially authoritarian and triumphalistic character of this approach to christological dogma meant that the teaching of the church functioned as, and was experienced as, anti-Jewish, patriarchal,[78] and imperialistic. As such, it contained no credibility of its own. It could not last.

Recovering the Jewish Matrix

Today, we continue to be tempted to think of Jesus as a kind of Greek God—someone such as a Superman character or a western hero. In his book, *Hunting the Divine Fox*, theologian Robert Farrar Capon describes our "temptation to jazz up the humanity of Christ." He writes:

> The true paradigm of the ordinary American view of Jesus is Superman: "Faster than a speeding bullet, more powerful than a locomotive, able to leap tall buildings in a single bound. It's Superman! Strange visitor from another planet, who came to earth with powers and abilities far beyond those of mortal men, and who, disguised as Clark Kent, mild-mannered reporter for a great metropolitan newspaper, fights a never-ending battle for truth, justice and the American way." If that isn't popular christology, I'll eat my hat. Jesus—gentle, meek and mild, but with secret, souped-up, more-than-human insides—bumbles around for thirty-three years, nearly gets himself done in for good by the Kryptonite Kross, but at the last minute, struggles into the phone booth of the Empty Tomb, changes into his Easter suit and, with a single bound, leaps back up to the planet Heaven. . . .

> You think that's funny? Don't laugh. The human race is, was and probably always will be deeply unwilling to accept a human messiah. We don't want to be saved in our humanity; we want to be fished out of it. We crucified Jesus, not because he was God, but because he blasphemed: He claimed to be God and then failed to come up to our standards for assessing the claim. It's not that we weren't looking for the Messiah; it's just that he

wasn't what we were looking for. Our kind of Messiah would come down from a cross. He wouldn't carry a folding phone booth in his back pocket. He wouldn't do a stupid thing like rising from the dead. He would do a smart thing like never dying.

If you don't believe me, look at the whole tradition of messiah figures in popular fiction. Superman is a classic but there are others just as good—and one that's even better—for illustrating our hunger for a nonhuman messiah. How about the sheriff in the typical "salvation" Western? Matt Dillon can be wounded but not killed, daunted but never defeated. . . .

Ditto the Lone Ranger, heigh-hoing around the days of yesteryear with Tonto, a white horse, no women, and a beltful of silver bullets. . . .

Not convinced yet? That's because I haven't given you the clincher. These Western sheriffim are a little misleading. They still, like Superman, have the appearance of humanity. It is not until we come to the ultimate popular messiah figure that we realize how much we despise our nature: We are so desperate to get rid of it that our imaginations will accept not only superhuman messiahs, but subhuman ones, too. . . . (In "Lassie"), (l)ittle Timmie goes schlepping all over the countryside getting himself lost, strayed or stolen, but he's practically the only human character in the show. Mother and Father are a couple of clowns who couldn't keep track of the movements of Mount Rushmore. . . . But no matter. Lassie *vincit omnia*. She will be beaten by bad men, bitten by alligators, clawed by mountain lions, and left for dead in the desert. But three days later! Home she comes with the snow goose on her back, the ailing poodle in an improvised litter, and in her mouth, Mother's wedding ring, Father's wallet, and a note to pick up Timmie at the supermarket.[798]

We must not take what *we think* God is—according to some Greek notions that to be a god, God must be supernatural (infinite, immortal, impassible, and unmoved or untouched by the world) to evaluate whether or not Jesus fits that definition. When we try to turn Jesus into some version of Superman,[80] or apply supernatural attributes to Jesus, we compromise the historical Jesus: the Jesus revealed through God's involvement in history. However, if we want to understand what God is doing in the world, we must recover the Jewish matrix out of which arose the confession that Jesus is Lord. Unlike the Greeks, the people of Israel understood that the difference between God and humankind is not primarily about ontology or beingness; it was and is about a turning point in history, in which the resurrection of Jesus reveals God's capacity for infinite unconditional love and compassion. It is about the constant faithfulness *of God* throughout history, despite the repeated failings of God's people. It is this faithfulness of God that makes God worthy of trust both for ancient Israelites and for us today.

Martin Luther discusses the idea of "god" in his explanation to the first commandment in his *Large Catechism*:

> Question: What is it to have a god?

> Answer: A god is that to which we look for all good and in which we find refuge in every time of need. To have a god is nothing else than to trust and believe (him) with our whole heart.[81]

As I have often said, the trust and faith of the heart alone make both God and an idol. The issue for Luther is whether or not, in claiming a "god," we have encountered that which is truly trustworthy; or if, by contrast, we have attached ourselves to "an idol."

Recall from Chapter 1 that Kant, who is recognized for his discussion of the nature and limits of human knowledge, affirmed the centuries-old argument that we have no access to a supernatural "god." He pointed out that we cannot "know" a being which is abstract and provides no sensory or experiential information.

Two hundred years later, significant theological moves were offered by Paul Tillich (1886-1965). Tillich was a twentieth-century German-born theologian who spent much of his adult life in the United States. His primary area of interest was an analysis of the forms of culture, and, as such, he sought a religious dimension in all cultural activities. Following Martin Luther's approach to the concept of "god," Tillich identified "god" not in terms of the supernatural, but in terms of "ultimacy," and claimed that "god" means whatever is one's "ultimate concern." This approach allows both Kant's foci on experience (of having an ultimate concern) and a cognitive structure (the meaning of ultimacy) through which "god" can be known. It also addresses Luther's concern about attaching oneself to "an idol," for it is possible to regard as ultimate that which cannot bear the weight of ultimacy. The fact that we can commit ourselves ultimately does not mean that there is anyone or anything which can bear the weight of ultimacy. It may be that if death has the last word, our Christian faith in God's ultimacy will fail us.[82]

The Gospels function to interpret "the history of Jesus as the history of God with the world."[83] This means that we apply what we know about Jesus to God. We pay attention to God's resurrection of Jesus as the basis for the confession that Jesus is God. That is what the disciples did. They understood Jesus' resurrection to be an eschatological event with proleptic character. The point was not only that Jesus has death behind him, or that "death no longer has dominion over him;"[84] indeed, the point was—and is—that Jesus' resurrection discloses the *outcome* of history in the *midst* of history—and the outcome is that God acts to redeem, to save all creation, not just on Easter Sunday, but on to this moment and all the next ones. That's why Jesus' resurrection is news yet today. In Jesus' resurrection we see the "last chapter" of history while we are still living out the "plot" of history.

We began this chapter with verses from Hosea 11:8-9 because the text emphasizes the depth of the divine love that will not forsake God's people. Admah and Zeboiim are cities that were destroyed with Sodom and Gomorrah. In remembering them, the text reveals the story of God's redeeming love—love which saves in ways beyond human understanding.

The historical mission of Jesus is the redemption of the creation, and it is to this topic that we turn next.

ISAIAH 52: 7-10

How beautiful upon the mountains

are the feet of the messenger who announces peace,

who brings good news, who announces salvation,

who says to Zion, "Your God reigns."

Listen! Your sentinels lift up their voices,

together they sing for joy; for in plain sight

they see the return of the Lord to Zion.

Break forth together into singing, you ruins of Jerusalem;

for the Lord has comforted his people, he has redeemed Jerusalem.

The Lord has bared his holy arm

before the eyes of all the nations;

and all the ends of the earth shall see the salvation of our God.

CHAPTER 3

THE HISTORICAL MISSION OF JESUS

"Your God reigns!"

The messenger makes his way down the mountainside, aware of the power of the words he will speak, for he knows how long the people of Israel have been waiting to hear them. The prospect of making this announcement fills him with anticipation. His feet ache from the long journey—but they are feet which have taken him from the Rock upon which the people of Israel have entrusted their lives, from the One True God.

He emerges from the mountain, panting, racing toward the Israelites. He sees the sentinels, and they see him. They notice the energy in his stride, and wonder: Could this be a sign of good news? They call out to the people: The messenger is coming!

The people see the messenger, too. He is advancing now through the grape vineyards, winding in and out of the olive groves. A crowd forms, and as the messenger sees them gathering, he knows he cannot stop to rest or to take a breath or to ease his bleeding and throbbing feet. He has the words they have been waiting for generations to hear! No longer will they think of themselves as "ruins of Jerusalem"—as mere remnant, second-rate cast-offs, rubble.

The people hold onto one another, anticipating, hoping. Could this be the moment? Indeed, how beautiful upon the mountains are the feet of the messenger—the messenger who comes in the name of the Lord—for he announces peace!

"Your God reigns!"

"Your God reigns!"

"Your God reigns!"

We can only imagine that they repeated these words over and over, sharing them with every member of the community: "Your God reigns!"

In one verse, Isaiah 52:7 reveals the innermost desire of the people of Israel: Peace, good news, and salvation are at hand because "Your God reigns!"

The task. We begin by discussing the function of history in a Jewish context, for it is through history that we begin to understand what is meant by the phrase "reign of God"[85]— what it meant to first-century Jews and what it means today. With this understanding in place, we will consider how Jesus' mission, actions, and claims were consistent with his proclamation of the coming reign of God.

The Function of History in the Jewish Context

To grasp the function of history—that is, to understand how history supports the claim that God is redeeming the creation—we need to imagine the mindset of first-century Israel. The Jewish understanding of time is not cyclical, but linear—a significant point of differentiation, for the people of Israel were surrounded by whole cultures which operated with a cyclical understanding of time. For example, Eastern religions looked at time as a wheel; the concept of reincarnation is predicated on this approach to time. If you think of a wheel with compartments in it, then you would imagine that when you die, you may graduate from a lower compartment to a higher compartment. Your next incarnation, if you're lucky, may be to a higher incarnation than the one you are currently in. For example, you, too, could be born with the life of someone like a Donald Trump. Or a Dallas Cowboy. Whew! However, the best consequence would be to be spun off the wheel of cyclical history altogether so that you would not be subject to another incarnation. So cyclical and linear concepts of time have importance when we want to understand history.

From the perspective of the people of Israel, time is linear, but it is not infinite. Instead of going on into some sort of oblivion or void, linear time has a beginning and moves towards a *telos*—that is, a consummation, an outcome, a definitive end. As time moves toward its outcome, we can identify this process as "history."

History allows us to say that events are experienced by, or occur in the midst of, a community. This community becomes, or is reinforced, by virtue of the shared experience of these events. The community receives and also hands on the shared events in terms of cognitive structures which provide "understanding." Story is one of those cognitive structures. Story tells about an event in a particular way, paying attention to some details and leaving out others. Which details are mentioned? The ones that the community understands to be important are shared and passed on to the next generation and again, to the next. The ways the community understands certain ideas—the way it identifies "givens" for example—show the categories it has established for organizing and defining events that come along in its history.

In U.S. history, we might say that the Civil War is an event that happened to some of the people who lived on the continent that now makes up the United States of America. Garry Wills makes a powerful case for the fact that in the Gettysburg Address, Abraham Lincoln reinvented America, for there is, in fact, nothing in the original documents of this country—this community—which justifies the kind of sweeping vision that this president articulated in his speech. Today we automatically accept Lincoln's vision; it's not even debated. Wills says Lincoln was quite conscious of what he was doing, and some who heard and understood it didn't like it. *The Chicago Tribune*, for example, wrote a harsh critique of the Gettysburg Address, saying that Lincoln was changing the Constitution, and with that, he was changing the whole conception of what America is: Nowhere in the original Constitution is there any claim that this is a land dedicated to the proposition that all human beings are created equal. Slaves were not regarded as persons. They had no rights. But Lincoln's address articulated a different vision: that those who gave their lives were sacrificing them for a certain ideal. Lincoln focused his argument very carefully and articulated it in such a way that none of us question it anymore.[86]

Something dramatic also occurs in the event of Jesus[87]—and our understanding of that event is the basis of our faith. The linear nature of time—that it moves toward a *telos*—is the essential point here. The events of Jesus' life, crucifixion, and resurrection occurred in a particular place and at a particular time. We know they happened in human history. As such, the narrative of these events is the Christian community's "story." We continue to live "in" this story, so that the story informs the meaning of our lives, and guides how we live them out.

The history of the people of Israel tells of their relationship with God and their relationships among one another. A secondary history might be thought of as their history as a nation. Likewise, U.S. history can be told in a variety of ways to define the nation, its policies, and its people. The historical account as told by Ronald Reagan is instructive here. Reagan selected certain events out of our past. He said we came to this empty land, and we conquered it by our own efforts. Then he built on that foundation by claiming that in the latter days of the twentieth century, government had taken away from us the just rewards of our hard work and our enterprise. He challenged people to support him in taking their destiny back from the government and to get the government off their backs: Do you recognize that narrative? It is highly selective. Just for starters, the land was not empty. Furthermore, it was through successive ways of exploiting people that this country was built.

Contrast Reagan's point of view with, say, that of a labor organizer. This person might tell our country's story using a very different set of events. For example, the organizer might say the truth is that we didn't just pull ourselves up by our own bootstraps, but that we relied on indentured servants from England: People bought their ways out of debtors prisons by giving their labor for seven or ten years to somebody in the Colonies who would ship them over. We relied on forced and involuntary slavery of African-Americans. Chinese laborers built the railroads for poor wages and hardly any respect for their lives. Irish immigrants were exploited by the people who arrived in this country before them; they determined to get their revenge by becoming politically effective and successful—and with that energy, they reinvented Boston.

People from Finland were exploited by the people from Sweden who put them into mining and other labor; they gathered more around the union halls than around the churches to which their Swedish masters belonged. One can trace waves of people who were exploited by their predecessors, people who happened to have squatters' rights.

The second version of the American story selects a *different* set of events, and weaves them into a narrative that also is coherent, but probably less politically marketable. We would much rather believe Reagan's story. Huge numbers of us loved it. The question is whether or not it is *true*.

The quest for a true story. The community's story can be true—or it can be false and destructive. An example of a false and destructive story is the German narrative that made the Nazi hegemony possible. Adolph Hitler claimed that a Jewish conspiracy was undermining the right of a superior Nordic race with a plan to dominate Europe and then the world. He told that story with consummate power and enormous rhetorical skill, and he seized a moment in German and European history when he thought he could make people believe it. The Holocaust was not an aberration in the Nazi philosophy; it was its *telos* or goal. And Hitler diverted enormous resources to exterminate the Jews. The events which made up the Nazi plot were not accidental; they were essential to his plan. Nazism was racist to the core and based on the notion that the German race, the Nordic race, had a right to enslave people in Eastern Europe and exterminate Jews. Hitler also showed his contempt for so-called "mongrel cultures" where racial purity no longer prevailed—and this attitude was the reason why he did not fear the U.S. entry into World War II.

The events that occurred at Auschwitz symbolize the extreme to which self-deception can lead. The complicity of Christians with Auschwitz did not begin with failure to object to the first slightly anti-Semitic laws and actions. It began when Christians assumed that they could be the heirs and carriers of symbols of their faith without sacrifice. It began when the very language of revelation became an expression of status rather than an instrument for bringing our lives gradually under the sway of "the love that moves the sun and the other stars."[88] Persons had come to call themselves Christians, and yet they lived as though they could avoid suffering and death. They were seized by powers that they no longer had the ability to know, much less to combat.[89] Their understanding of the Christian story had been subverted and corrupted.

Stanley Hauerwas says we need a "true story," for only a true story would be

> powerful enough to check the endemic tendency toward self-deception—a tendency which inadequate stories cannot help but foster. . . . If the true God were to provide us with a saving story, it would have to be one that we found continually discomforting. For it would be a saving story only as it empowered us to combat the inertial drift into self-deception.[90]

The quest for the true story can be a daunting task—but we take it on, realizing that we can distinguish truths even in the midst of the brokenness of the human condition.

Ultimacy revealed in outcome. History invites us to ask questions of meaning in terms of our "story." We can experience the provisional falsity of a communal story in terms of provisional outcomes, such as the falsity of the Nazi story in terms of the revelations during and subsequent to the Nazi era of 1933 to 1945. In the midst of the unfolding of this story, as Hitler came into power, he quickly began to do certain things which would reveal, if a person had any discernment at all, the essential deceptiveness of his story. We can look at the last weekend of June and the first day of July 1934. Hitler carried out during the Night of the Long Knives a swift purge of about a thousand people, some in their cells, some in their homes. They opened their doors to bursts of machine gun fire; in an instant, they were dead. That's what happened to the former prime minister of Germany, Chancellor General Kurt von Schleicher and his wife Elisabeth. Ernst Röhm, who was the head of the Brownshirts, was murdered in his bed. Hitler went on the air to announce that at this moment of supreme crisis, he had to be judge, jury, and executioner for the German nation. People bought it. But those who didn't accept that version of the Night of the Long Knives could begin to understand the speciousness of the overarching story it was meant to endorse, even as it was unfolding in their midst.

Provisional truth also can be experienced. For example, Abraham Lincoln's commitment to the end of slavery is a story that was provisionally true; Lincoln achieved it by means of making the freeing of the slaves an instrument of war. The Emancipation Proclamation did not come as a kind of general statement about slavery because it affected only slaves in states still in rebellion. So Lincoln freed slaves as an act of war. Were alternatives possible? Well, that's a very interesting historical question. Could the slaves have been freed as an economic act instead of as an act of military policy? Well, it wasn't done that way, so who knows?

Ultimate truth or final authentic historical meaning is known only from a story's final end, its ultimate outcome. We can ask about the ripples of Abraham Lincoln's policies. We are still paying for the decision to use military policy to free slaves: The need for a Civil Rights movement to continue the struggle is part of that payment; the unmet need for economic justice for Blacks in this country is another. We do not know the full and final outcome of that military policy.

I also might use myself as an example of the ultimacy of truth. I do not know the outcome of what I teach. I do not know its ripples, where they will go, what effect my teaching will have because I am not in control of your biographies, your destinies, your stories. I don't know what you will do with my work, and the people who are in my classes are going to do different things with what I teach! So the final outcome of my enterprise will not be known when I retire or when I die. It may not be known when you retire or die. It will be known when all the people whom you teach and all the people whom they teach—well, when history reaches its *telos*. In other words, the final consequence of what I am engaged in, what we are engaged in, is going to be known only at the end. Because we are in the midst of history, we can know ultimate meaning only if the outcome is given to us.

The Christian story is based on the truth that one such outcome *is* given to us. The *revelation* of the final outcome of history, according to the Gospel, has taken place *in history*: Jesus of Nazareth is raised from the dead and is the Christ. God's salvation is not about an *escape from time* but rather is the *promise* of God's final future to all who are *in* time. The grounds for God's salvation promise was announced through an event which happened in time—in and through Jesus. This grounding is not a *general* claim for religious truth. It is about something quite *specific*: Jesus is Messiah. The reign of God has been inaugurated.

Your God Reigns

Thus far, we have said that the Christian story is based on the good news that Jesus of Nazareth is resurrected (Chapter 1), and that Jesus is God (Chapter 2). The story of the Christian faith continues with the claim that through the resurrection of Jesus, God began the process of redeeming the creation. Since salvation is good news—news which continues to be revealed to us today—and since Jesus is God, we now must ask what is meant by the announcement, "Your God reigns."

Unpacking Isaiah 52:7-10. To understand what Jesus meant by his announcement that "(t)he time is fulfilled, and the Kingdom of God has come near" (Mark 1:14), is to consider the meaning of the expression "your God reigns" from the perspective of first-century Jews. They would have connected the two texts immediately, for the writings of the prophets were well known among the people of Israel. As we join in their understanding, we learn about a messenger who brings the good news that the people yearn to hear. It is an announcement of peace, good news, and salvation breaking into their midst. The text reveals their hope for the return of God.

The writings of the prophets did not stand alone. They often referred to other well-known stories and expressions that were common among the people of their time. Wright asserts that "(t)he messenger (of Isaiah 52:7) is the anointed of the spirit about whom Daniel spoke. . . ."[91] He continues:

> The vision in Daniel 2 concerns the kingdom of God and its
> triumph over the kingdoms of the world. . . . The "stone"
> which smashed the clay feet and which then became a huge

mountain was fairly certainly read as messianic by some groups in the first century, not least, perhaps, because of the well-known play between "stone" (*eben* in Hebrew) and "son" (*ben*). . . .[92]

When we consider Isaiah 52:7-10 with these insights, we glimpse the meaning of the Daniel text[93] from the perspective of first-century Judaism: Jesus' proclamation reveals the stone/son who is to prevail over an enemy. This use of "mountain" easily might refer to the prophets; a "huge mountain" would be a prophet—and more! So a first-century interpretation points to the truth the people of Israel have waited so long to hear: Jesus is both the messenger and the stone. He will overcome the enemy. He is the Messiah: Your God reigns!

Living in exile. In the first century, the people of Israel were under the rule of—that is, they were exiled under—the Romans. To be held in exile meant living as second-class people: a nation within a nation, existing as a separate community, but as mere rubble. They were captives in their own land. As such, they looked to God to redeem them from their affliction, just as God had done so many times before—against the Assyrians and, later, against the Babylonians.

Why had God turned away from the people of Israel? Because they had not kept their covenant with God to live as a light to other nations. It had happened many times. Then, about 100 years before the birth of Jesus, a religious movement called the Pharisees formed and gained some favor with the chief priests in the temple. The Pharisees admonished the people of Israel to rigorously follow Torah. They contended that if the people were pure, Yahweh would return and vindicate them—that is, God would show all of the nations that the God of the people of Israel was the One True God, and that they, then, were God's chosen people. God would lift them from exile and return them to their rightful place among nations.

It was when this Pharisaic vision was in full flower that Jesus came and announced that the long wait being experienced by the people of Israel was about to end. In proclaiming God's intentions, Jesus referred to prophetic texts the people understood well: "Your God reigns!"

The mission. When the people of Israel used the phrase "reign of God," the words pointed to their hope that God would act to vindicate Israel. To them, God's reign referred to a state-of-being connected with freedom from exile and release from the rule of the enemy.

But the people of Israel had identified the wrong enemy.

The enemy whom God wanted exposed as powerless was not the Romans—or any other nation (for Jewish ancestors had been exiled many times before). No, God sought to expose the powerlessness *of death*.

Remember that God's plan for the creation is redemption. Through the resurrection of Jesus, God continues to be faithful to *God's original plan: that Israel was to be a light to the world*—that is, as chosen people, they were the means by which other nations would come to know and follow God. Once again, God forgave Israel for not keeping her covenant. The exile was over—even though the Romans continued to run the country.

Here it is important for us to understand that everything Jesus does and teaches is pursuant to God's plan to redeem the creation. That is, Jesus described his mission in terms of the reign of God, decisively present in all he said and all he did. The way he lived his mission implied that the reign of God had a specific content and character. Moreover, the nature of the reign of God as Jesus taught and manifested it pushed beyond the traditional Jewish beliefs about what would actually happen when their God reigned. In *Jesus and the Victory of God*, Wright proposes what he calls "the double criterion of similarity and dissimilarity" as a foundation for explaining how the New Testament writings serve as credible historical witnesses on how Jesus' ministry both affirmed and transformed Jewish thought regarding what the reign of God was all about:

> When something can be seen to be credible (though perhaps deeply subversive) within first-century Judaism, *and* credible as the implied starting point (though not the exact replica) of something in later Christianity, there is a strong possibility of our being in touch with the genuine history of Jesus.[94]

To be credible as founded in fact, Wright says that the Jesus of history must be intelligible within a Jewish context, yet challenging enough to be crucified. The Jesus of history must also explain the messianic movement which followed his crucifixion and eventuated in the church. The historian must give an account of Jesus which is historically plausible enough to account for the move from first-century Judaism to first-century Christianity. That account must include the messianic character of Jesus' own claims, sayings, deeds, and destiny.

By the most stringent criteria, the minimum historically probable material mediated by the Gospels includes Jesus' table collegiality with sinners, the parables and the Lord's Prayer tradition, and the crucifixion. Despite significant variations in the details and despite differing perspectives in proclamation, most of the traditions preserved in the Gospels have a basis in fact as to what Jesus said and did. Conclusions from Arland Hultgren are instructive here:

> In regard to the question whether a given type of redemptive christology preserves continuity with what was most characteristic of the ministry of Jesus, it is necessary to preface the discussion with a crisp indication of what can be considered most characteristic.
>
> . . . Jesus, the prophet of the kingdom, revealed the nature of the messianic kingdom by acting out the role of one who embodies the features of life in the messianic kingdom, representing the kingdom proleptically to his contemporaries. In this regard it can be said that he was more than a prophet of the kingdom. For as one who represented the kingdom to others by his own words and deeds, and who embodied in his own life the features of the kingdom, he was a figure standing on the boundary between this world and the kingdom to come. And although he was a flesh-and-blood person in this world, it was possible for those who followed him to

perceive a transcendent quality in him and to regard him as one who was destined already to have a leading role, and therefore a preeminence, in the kingdom to come. He acted with divine authority to forgive sins and declare salvation to others—persons who then went away believing that they had forgiveness and salvation.

In so doing, Jesus freed men and women by assuming to himself the burden of sins and their consequences; he acted as one who was answerable to God for others, and who expected the vindication of his actions by God. And the vindication of his actions would certify that he had truly acted on God's behalf, that God was in him, liberating and reconciling the estranged to himself.

He went on to accept crucifixion on the basis of the charge of being the Messiah, a charge which he did not reject. To put it as crisply as we can, Jesus so identified with a redefined messianic role that the line of demarcation was worn away and even crossed; he was, in his own way, a redemptive, messianic figure. It is only a very small step from this for his disciples to understand later that his death and resurrection, considered as a unity, was redemptive as well. For after his death and resurrection his followers experienced both his presence among them and newness of life through the presence and power of the Spirit. . . .

The one who had assumed the burden of others in his historical ministry had assumed the burden of all people once and for all, for his resurrection and the pouring out of the spirit mark the beginning of the new age, which has universal, cosmic dimensions. The cross and resurrection event is so decisive and disruptive that the universe is no longer the same as it was previously. A new world has been opened up.[95]

It is our purpose here to flesh out Hultgren's "crisp indication of what can be considered most characteristic" of the mission of Jesus. The material thus identified indicates that Jesus' own claim about his mission and activity (that is, in him the eschatological reign of God has come) coincides with the church's authentic claim about him (that is, that he is the eschatological Messiah, the Christ as the crucified one).

Jesus as the Breaking In of the Redemptive Reign of God

Jesus' mission is characterized by the message that the redemptive reign of God is breaking into the world. In Mark 1:14-15, he proclaimed the good news of God, saying, "The time is fulfilled, and the kingdom of God has come near; repent, and believe in the good news." Here we want to remember that the concept of the "kingdom"—or "reign" of God—is given new content by Jesus. His message was *not* a reinforcement of a nationalistic expectation for the restoration of rule to Israel. Rather, the idea of reign is embodied in his messages and activities. We need to ask, "What did he say?" and "What did he do?" The account in Luke 17:20-21 is instructive:

> Once Jesus was asked by the Pharisees when the kingdom of God was coming and he answered, "The kingdom of God is not coming with things that can be observed; nor will they say, 'Look, here it is!' or 'There it is!' For, in fact, the kingdom of God is among you."

Then he says that if he, by the finger of God, is casting out demons, then the reign of God is in your midst! So don't look here . . . or there. . . . Rather, the reign is happening right in front of you, in what Jesus is up to.

Redemptive reign of God in the activity of Jesus. Luke 4:14-30 tells how Jesus began to preach about the reign of God in synagogues. In this text, he is given a scroll from the prophet Isaiah, and he reads from the sixty-first chapter, as Luke describes it—a very wonderful, dramatic account, beginning with verse 18:

> "The Spirit of the Lord is upon me,
> because he has anointed me to bring good news to the poor.
> He has sent me to proclaim release to the captives
> and recovery of sight to the blind,

to let the oppressed go free,
to proclaim the year of the Lord's favor."

And he rolled up the scroll, gave it back to the attendant, and
sat down. The eyes of all in the synagogue were fixed on him.

Of special significance is the reference to the "year of the Lord's favor."
This is so threatening that those who hear Jesus are filled with anger and
set out to kill him. Here we must ask, "What is it about the 'year of the
Lord' that is so upsetting?"

Most scholars think it is a reference to the jubilee year, the fiftieth
year, the one that is seven times seven years. And what was special about
that jubilee year? Described in Leviticus, it is when debts are forgiven
and property restored to its original owners. We don't know if it was
ever invoked in history—that is, if it ever actually happened—but the
very idea scared the money lenders. Rabbis tell us that a couple of years
before the fiftieth year would come along, nobody would lend money
anymore because they were afraid they wouldn't get it back—because
debts would be forgiven in the year of the Lord's favor.

When Jesus says, "Today these words are fulfilled in your ears," we
might want to ask why they didn't throw a party, light a bonfire, have a
celebration—a kegger, you know. Why not? Instead, those who heard
his reading rushed to get him—to throw him over a cliff. "Why?" we
ask. The reason is that the people who have a stake in the present—who
bought property that belonged to others, who enslaved fellow Jews, who
had debtors who owed them money—aren't interested in this cursed
jubilee year business! "Get out of here!" is what they would want to say.
That's what is going on in this text—and it's why they set out to kill him.

Reign of God as liberation of the oppressed. When John the Baptist was
in prison, he sent a message to Jesus, asking, "Are you ἐρχόμενος?"—
that is, "Are you the one to come?" And Jesus replied, "Go tell John what
you see and hear: the blind receive their sight, the lame walk, the lepers
are cleansed, the deaf hear, the dead are raised, and the poor have good
news brought to them. And blessed is anyone who takes no offense at
me."[96]

While the various acts of Jesus were significant, they were not unique to him. That is, Jesus is not the only one casting out demons. He is not the only one through whom the lame would walk, We recall that they sat by the pool, waiting for the angel to trouble the waters, so that whoever got down there first was going to be cured. Cures were known in the whole ancient world. All of these things were happening. So to assert that Jesus could be *proven* to be *divine* by his miracles is nonsense. In refutation of such an idea, he says, "Don't tell me that I am casting out demons in the name of the prince of demons. If I do that, by whom do your sons cast them out?"[97]

The point to be made here is that when Jesus healed the sick or re-suscitated the dead, his actions were *signs*: signs of the breaking in of the redemptive reign of God. Moltmann says:

> Healings and salvation are related to one another in such a way that the *healings* are signs, this side of death, of God's power of the resurrection or, as John says, signs of Christ's "glory"; while salvation is the fulfillment of these prefigured real promises in the raising of the dead to eternal life. Just as healing overcomes sickness, so salvation overcomes death. Because every sickness is a threat to life, and is therefore a foreshadowing of death, every healing is a living foretoken of the resurrection. . . .
>
> Salvation in this sense has two sides to it, one *personal* and one *cosmic*. Paul calls the personal side of salvation "the resurrection of the dead." He calls the cosmic side "the anni-hilation of death." It is only if we see the two sides together that we understand that salvation also means "the transfig-uration of the body" (Philippians 3:21) and "the new earth" (Revelation 21:4). These two aspects can also be perceived in Jesus' own healings: healing the sick is the personal side; driving out demons is the cosmic side. Sick people are sub-jectively healed; they are made free and well. At the same time the world is objectively de-demonized; the bacilli that cause these possessions are destroyed. Jesus heals the sick

and symbolically liberates creation from the powers of destruction, which at that time were called "demons."[98]

So Jesus' healings are signs that God has again returned to Israel in Jesus' own ministry.

God's unconditional affirmation of the lost sheep. Jesus' proclamation and activity point to the coming reign of God as understood in terms of Ezekiel 34:1-24, a text in which God castigates the false shepherds and promises that "I myself will search for my sheep," that "I will set up over them one shepherd, my servant David, and he shall feed them." Here it is clear that the redemptive reign of God began with the renewal of Israel through the surprise of God's unconditional affirmation of the "lost sheep of the house of Israel."

What in the world is that about? They are the sinners and the tax collectors—people who don't count, you see—at least not with regard to the political expectations of first-century Israel.[99] In various ways, these people had been alienated or had alienated themselves.

But God's affirmation of them was neither indulgent (the affirmation did not say, "Do whatever you want"), nor exploitative (it did not suggest, "How can I use you?")—because you can't use women and children in a political revolution. This is especially offensive because it calls into question the Pharisaic expectation that Messiah would set up a kingdom "in place of that of the Gentiles and sinners."[100] But Jesus claims that God is establishing a reign that accepts people who are alienated, sinners, Romans, and their lackey tax collectors. He says, "I am sent to the lost sheep of the house of Israel," and in this announcement, he is directly countering the Pharisaic messianic expectation.

In these many ways, his lordship was qualitatively different from all others. His was the lordship of life, not the lordship of death; his was the lordship of the future, not of brute power over other nations. In this, he clashes with powerful factions in Israel whose opinions about how to fulfill God's will were far different. The Pharisees' focus was to maintain purity while in exile, the Zealots focused on armed revolt, and the chief priests and the Sadducees focused on collaborating with the Romans to maintain the status quo. Jesus challenges them all.

Re-appropriating the Story

In Chapter 1, we said that "to re-appropriate is to retake possession of—and here, it is to reclaim an idea, and to do so with authority." Through words and actions, Jesus re-appropriated—or redefined, retold, and corrected—the common narrative described in the history of the people of Israel. Torah takes on new meaning through Jesus' teaching. And parables reinterpret long-held assumptions by giving expected endings a new twist.

New "torah". The redemptive reign of God initiates a new or renewed "torah"—that is, a new or renewed "way" to be—in service and witness to the reign of God.[101] Each of the five books is reinterpreted in this light. First, the blessing to Abraham in Genesis is extended to the poor, the meek, and so on. We see it in Matthew 5:1-16, which includes "Blessed are the poor in spirit. . . ." If one understands that the whole *point* of Genesis is the blessing of Abraham *through whom all nations* will be blessed, then we have a magnification of that expression in the Beatitudes.

Secondly, the covenantal decalogue of the Exodus is renewed. Here we refer to Matthew 5:17-48, which addresses concerns about consistency or clarity between Jesus' message and Jewish law. At first he says, "Do not think that I have come to abolish the law or the prophets . . ." as a way of affirming the scrolls as they were given. Then, beginning in verse 21, he begins to reinterpret—that is, to correct in light of the reign of God—how these laws and the writings of the prophets are to be understood. The pattern is recognizable: "You have heard that it was said to those of ancient times . . ." and Jesus repeats the law. *"But I say to you . . ."* introduces his reinterpretation, and he continues with the new and acceptable teaching. Murder, adultery, truth-telling, and so on: Jesus provided numerous examples of how the texts are to be correctly understood with the coming of the reign of God.

Matthew 6:1-18, which opens with "Beware of practicing your piety before others in order to be seen by them," can be thought of as a reworking of the worship legislation of Leviticus. Here Jesus renews ideas about giving alms, prayer, and fasting.

Next, as Israel's strength is not in its numbers but in God, so is the reign of God to be characterized by trust in God's care. Matthew 6:19-34 contrasts the lilies of the field (which have only God to care for them) with David's census and numbering of the people. Instead of flexing muscle, Jesus says the people of Israel should trust God. Finally, as God set before Israel the choice between death and life, and Israel is to choose life,[102] so the reign of God is like building one's house on rock. Matthew 7:1-27 provides numerous examples of the practical meaning of Jesus' message.

Jesus interprets his activity in parables. Jesus uses parable to reveal what he is doing and to reshape the worldview of his followers. It is helpful here to understand something about the story typology that is particular to the parable. Parable is the opposite of myth. Myth establishes a particular understanding of the world. For example, we continue to tell stories about the honesty of George Washington and Honest Abe to perpetuate the worldview that Americans and the nation's leaders are good and admirable people.

By contrast, Bornkamm says, "The Gospels are the rejection of myth."[103] Stories which function in the Gospel to *subvert misguided perceptions* of the world are parables. A cartoon example is helpful here. *Peanuts* characters often lead us to bring to mind one set of expectations, then surprise us with a revelatory twist. My version of a *Peanuts* cartoon strip would show someone—let's say Lucy—announcing, "I want to go to seminary. I want to learn about everything and everyone in the Bible, all about St. Paul . . ." and then in the next box she would say, "and Minneapolis!" Got you! Right? We could have gone on and said, "St. Paul and St. Peter and St. John . . ." and we'd have been in a flow. But with parable you get this little twist—this time it's with Minneapolis, and you're hooked because your expectations have been radically revised. Your idea of what seminary study is about would be changed!

Now let's look at the Gospels. Matthew 20:1-16 is the story of the laborers in the vineyard, and in it we see the tension that erupts when everyone receives the same wage—whether they worked all day or only one hour. Jesus' listeners already knew one version of this narrative, because it was a common story in the first century. In it, a young rabbi died, and all of his rabbinic colleagues gathered for the funeral. An elderly rabbi who preached the sermon said they should not mourn the death of their young colleague because he accomplished as much in his brief lifespan as they will accomplish in their much longer ones.[104] Now, the story of the laborers in the vineyard sets up a similar conflict. Following the pattern in the story of the young rabbi would suggest that the workers who spent only one hour in the field accomplished as much as the ones who were out in the sun all day. Merit would be based on the number of baskets each brought in, not on the time it took to do the work. But Jesus leads them to the edge where he offers an unanticipated twist. The ending of the story as he tells it is not about the number of hours *or* the number of baskets—but on the generosity of God. In verse 15, the owner of the vineyard says, "Am I not allowed to do what I choose with what belongs to me?" In other words, he asks, "Do you begrudge my generosity?" By way of contrast, some of Jesus' listeners might have expected the twist to be "I can smash my own"—just as we see in *Crime and Punishment*: A drunkard comes out of a tavern and beats his horse to death. When his friends shout at him, "Stop beating the horse!" he replies, "I can do what I want with my own." But God doesn't do this—and there is the twist: When God says, "I can do what I want with my own," it is to be generous, to be merciful. The parable is not about merit or about what people accomplish, for the truth is that the people of Israel could not earn the one thing God sought. They had broken their covenant and failed in their vocation to be a light to the world. But Jesus provides an unexpected ending to his parable: God is merciful.

With parable, Jesus recreates the story of the people of Israel, then shows the ending God has had in mind. The reign of God is radically different in the telling that Jesus provides. The same stories are re-appropriated, so they are consistent with the reign of God—and this is why history is important to understanding who we are as Christians. We do not just *tell* stories; we *live in* story.[105] We understand ourselves in terms of our own "script," which refers to the life-story we tell about ourselves, in the way we think, and in all we say and all we do. Likewise, Jesus' parables were intended to break open the world redemptively. Or, as John Dominic Crossan says, "Parables give God room."[106]

Parable reinterpreted the way the people of Israel understood God's purposes for the world. Through these reinterpretations, they came to link the reign of God with the coming of the eschatological banquet.[107] You also can look at the connection between the reign of God and the risk of grace in the parable of the dishonest steward, as told in Luke 16:1-7. Stewards were paid in commissions. When this crooked steward finally figures out that he's about to get fired, instead of going to collect his commission (which is what you do: maybe you'll have enough to go to the Bahamas or something like that), he goes to each of the tenants he has cheated, and he says, "Knock my commission off your rent." With that move, he is utterly at their mercy. Now we have to ask: What do you *do* with this crazy parable about the dishonest steward?

Look at the order in which these parables appear in the biblical text. Luke 15 starts with the story of the lost sheep,[108] next is the one about the lost coin,[109] and then the one about the two sons.[110] You can see that in each of them, the main characters—the shepherd, the woman, and the father—are still in charge. No matter how good the outcome, they're in charge.

But the ultimate parable is the one about dishonest steward, for the steward is utterly at the mercy of the people whose commissions he has cancelled. The enormously surprising twist here is that the "dishonest steward" in this parable represents God! And here we see Jesus saying that God's ultimate offering is to be at our mercy, to give up everything for the sake of the others, and then see what they will do in response. That's what it means.

Jesus also shows how the reign of God frees us for communal commitment.[111] Luke 14:16-24 is the parable about a feast, which is a communal event that carries with it a communal responsibility. When you kill an animal, you first send around a message to make sure everyone will be there to eat it, because you have no refrigeration. If the people who said they would come to eat don't show up, they're violating the community. They're not just rude; they're destructive! Why? Because everyone needs to eat. That's the way it works. So in Luke 14, when the invited guests don't show up at the appointed time for the meal, the owner of the house tells his servant to go into the streets and bring in the poor, the crippled, the blind and the lame. And when there is still room at the table, he orders his servant to compel all people to come in "so that my house may be filled."

In this parable and many of the others, we see Jesus' appeal for justice—for the world to be as God intended it to be—especially for persons who are poor. His announcement of the reign of God appeals to the universal calling of Israel in Abraham and in the prophets. He calls to the people of Israel to be an instrument of God's peace, hence his reference to forgiving enemies and to providing comfort to persons in prison. Matthew 25: 34-36 shows what he means with regard to Israel's calling to compassion:

> Then the king will say to those at his right hand, "Come, you that are blessed by my Father, inherit the kingdom prepared for you from the foundation of the world; for I was hungry and you gave me food, I was thirsty and you gave me something to drink, I was a stranger and you welcomed me, I was naked and you gave me clothing. I was sick and you took care of me. I was in prison and you visited me.

In this text, and many others, Jesus' intent was to help the people of Israel re-envision their original calling—a vocation of compassion, of being a light to the world, so that everyone would know the One True God. Stories were not about dividing one another into groups of those who were "saved" from those who were "damned" for all eternity. Eternity was not the issue! It is the *present* that is at stake. The time Jesus intended in Mark 1:14 was the exact moment of his telling. He was re-calling Israel to its vocation. The exile was ended.

"Your God reigns!"

1 CORINTHIANS 1: 23-25

Epistle of St. Paul

We proclaim Christ crucified,

a stumbling block to Jews and foolishness to Gentiles,

but to those who are the called, both Jews and Greeks,

Christ the power of God and the wisdom of God.

For God's foolishness is wiser than human wisdom,

and God's weakness is stronger than human strength.

CHAPTER 4

THE *SKANDALON* OF THE CROSS: THE CRUCIFIED MESSIAH

We begin this chapter with the claim that Jesus of Nazareth was and is Messiah.

Messiah is term of Jewish origin. Among the people of Israel, the term "son of God" could carry messianic connotations without necessarily referring to divine beingness. The word simply means "anointed one," and all of Israel's kings (when Israel had kings) had been anointed and were therefore "messiahs." Ever since the return from the Babylonian exile (597-538 B.C.), Jewish hopes for a restored kingdom—with an anointed king—had waxed and waned. Hope was once again waxing strong. This Messiah would be a great leader who would rescue the people of Israel from their exile—this time under the Romans. He would be wise and powerful; he would be a Son of God.

He would not be the son of a carpenter from out-of-the-way Nazareth in Lower Galilee. And he certainly would not be crucified on a cross! For Jews to conceive of the Messiah as One who died the death of a common criminal—well, they wouldn't think it! Such an idea would be a *skandalon*—or stumbling block—to their notions of God's participation in the world. For those looking for a David-like king, Jesus' claim to being the messiah made no sense.

As for the Corinthians (and others to whom Paul directed his ministry), such an idea might have appeared as pure foolishness. The Hellenistic world understood vicarious death. In August 480 B.C., King Leonidas of Sparta, prevented by political squabbling from sending his 300-man army to defend the narrow pass of Thermopylae, set out with his personal bodyguard to fight off the ambitious Persian king Xerxes. They gave their lives to buy time for the Greek armies to get together and eventually defeat their enemies: That makes sense in the Hellenistic world!

But would the Greeks accept the event of the cross? Would a Greek god participate in vicarious death? Remember that in Chapter 2 we said the Hellenistic view of "god" barred attributes which were material, concrete, or sensory. Certainly the experience of death while nailed onto a wooden cross contradicts a Greek interpretation of a deity. Indeed, Martin Hengel points out that the Corinthians already knew that this "Christ" had suffered a death which usually was reserved for hardened criminals and rebels against the Roman state. "That the crucified Jew, Jesus Christ, could truly be a divine being sent on earth, God's Son, the Lord of all and the coming judge of the world, must inevitably have been thought by any educated man to be utter 'madness' and presumptuousness."[112]

Major obstacles faced any Jew or Greek with the temerity to claim Jesus was the Messiah. For us, now some 2,000 years later, the seemingly paradoxical confession of a crucified Messiah belongs to "data which virtually everyone would consider historical." Hultgren makes the case that:

> The earthly Jesus was crucified under the authority of Pontius Pilate as a messianic pretender—regardless of how Jesus might have interpreted his own role—as indicated above all by the charter and inscription "King of the Jews" (Mark 15:26; Matt. 27:37; Luke 23:38; John 19:19). This formulation could not have risen out of early Christian theologizing or apologetics, since early Christians would have hesitated to apply such a title to Jesus because of its political consequences for the Christian movement itself and since it is the most fitting charge to explain the crucifixion of Jesus under Roman rule.[113]

Hultgren is saying that it would not have even occurred to early Christians to make up such an outrageous tale of a crucified Messiah. And if it had occurred to them, it would have not been in their favor to proclaim it—and yet, proclaim it they did! In fact, the radical nature of the truth of the crucified Christ contributes to its credence today.

The question for us, then, as "those who are called"—that is, as followers of Christ—is how we arrive at our proclamation of a crucified Messiah. Our creeds, our statements of faith, take account of the *skandalon* that Jesus the Christ is the crucified Messiah.

The task. We have said that the starting point for christology is the resurrection. We also want to say that the starting point for the doctrine of God—how we understand God—is the cross! We make these claims about the doctrine of God from a Christian perspective; a general conception of God might go about this task in another way, but we're not looking for a general conception of God. For our understanding, we must look at why we pay attention to Jesus.

This chapter will discuss the historical mission of Jesus which led to his crucifixion. It will briefly outline the reality of crucifixion as practiced by the Romans, compare Roman crucifixion with the narrative of the Gospels, focus on key elements of the crucifixion as historical phenomena, and then look at how the cross is taken up in the faith and confession of Jesus' disciples—that is, consider the crucifixion of the Messiah as a saving event.

The Historical Mission of Jesus

We know that the resurrection led the disciple community to retrieve and pass on to others the tradition about Jesus. Here it is important to remember that when Jesus was crucified, the disciples fled! Three days later, when Jesus was resurrected, they realized that God had vindicated Jesus. With this realization, they looked back at what they obviously had misconstrued. The first element of the tradition to be retrieved was, of course, the crucifixion.

The disciples' initial proclamation was not about the cross. Rather, Jesus was proclaimed as having been raised from the dead. But the very fact of the proclamation cannot mean that he died as "righteous sufferer" or as martyred prophet—for then his resurrection would mean only vindication of himself and would not be the grounds of a saving message. In fact, though, something decisive had happened for Jesus' disciples and for the whole world.

If resurrection alone were the Gospel, then the manner of Jesus' death would not have mattered, even if Jesus had died of old age. Death at an old age raises no questions. People know what is happening. People wear out. Death comes. Life goes on. But Jesus died horribly, innocently, executed, rejected. How could this happen to God's Anointed One? That raises eyebrows! Therefore, the question about the significance of such a death had to be—and must continue to be—addressed.

Before we consider Gospel accounts of Jesus' trial and crucifixion, we need to address a preliminary question: Why was Jesus put to death?

The historical reasons for Jesus' death point to his ministry: He antagonized the Pharisees, he riled the chief priests, and he troubled the Romans. All three groups played a role in the events that led up to Jesus' trial and crucifixion, so we need to ask: What was Jesus doing that gave each of them such cause for alarm?

The power of symbolism. The Pharisees were interested in upholding Jewish traditions in the hope that God would end the exile. The chief priests relied on the power of their position in the Temple to maintain their authority. The Romans were well aware that their ability to exercise control and safeguard their own law and order relied upon their ability to suppress troublemakers. All three—Jewish traditions, Temple authority, and control—attained at least some power through symbolic interpretation.

Wright illustrates the emotional importance of symbolism when he says, "Tease someone about their nationality if you wish, provided you know them well and they are tolerant, but do not even think of burning their flag."[114] The flag is a symbol, and as such, it contains *meaning*; it holds power beyond the weft and weave of its threads, and you just don't meddle with it.

But Jesus did meddle with symbols. He attacked, both implicitly and explicitly, the traditional representations of the Jewish worldview. Again, Wright is instructive:

[H]e saw them not as bad in themselves but as out of date, belonging to the period before the coming of the kingdom and to be jettisoned now that the new day had dawned. More, the symbols of his own work were deeply provocative, implying at every point that Israel, the people of God, was being redefined in and around him and his work.[115]

Redefined how? Jesus' actions were aimed at the inauguration of the reign of God. An inauguration is a launch, or a beginning. Here Jesus was signaling a new beginning for the reign of God: a *new* way of understanding themselves as God's people—and as a result, a *new* way of being.

The Pharisees, however, held firm to a traditional Jewish identity. They emphasized purity as a defense against paganism: against forces that would, if not continually wrestled, encourage Jewish assimilation into the dominant culture. Like Jesus, they were concerned about the coming of God's reign—but their interpretation was in direct conflict with the view being signaled by Jesus' actions. These two views of God's purposes in the world were widely divergent from each other. One would have to give way.

The temple . . . and the upper room. Jesus' symbolic actions in the countryside certainly antagonized the Pharisees. Not only did Jesus disagree with their kingdom perspective; he also was gaining a considerable following among the people. The situation escalated in Jerusalem as his actions in the Temple threatened the chief priests. The Temple was the symbol of authority among the people of Israel, so in Mark 11: 15-19, when we see Jesus cleansing the temple, we know he is intentionally challenging that authority. He overturned tables of the moneychangers, and he would not allow people to carry animal sacrifices from the Court of the Gentiles into the temple. He said, "Is it not written, 'My house shall be called a house of prayer for all the nations'? And *you* have made it a den of robbers."

We want to ask, "Who is this 'you'? Who made the temple into a den of robbers?"

The text immediately continues, "And when the chief priests and the scribes heard it, they kept looking for a way to kill him; for they were afraid of him, because the whole crowd was spellbound by his teaching."

We see, then, that the clash with temple authorities was sufficient to have Jesus arrested and condemned. The Temple was the symbol of authority, so Jesus' attack on *it* was a challenge to the authority of the *chief priests*. These guardians of the law condemned Jesus as a "blasphemer." Indeed, Moltmann reminds us that Jesus was condemned as "a demagogic false Messiah."[116] Others concur, pointing out that Jesus not only insisted that God is merciful; he also proclaimed and acted out that mercy toward publicans and sinners with "sovereign freedom."[117]

Whether or not Moltmann is guilty of hyperbole and exaggerated dialectics, we can see that differences existed between Jesus and some of his powerful contemporaries over his implicit and explicit messianic claims and their messianic expectations. These differences came to a head in Jesus' clash with the temple authorities who asserted the sole right to interpret God's law; as such they also held the right to judge when the law was broken. Jesus' claims and actions were sufficient to allow Jewish authorities to arrest and condemn him.

We want to look at the symbolism of Jesus' actions. In attacking the temple, he pointed to what YHWH was about to accomplish with the inauguration of the kingdom: not piety, not sacrifice, but forgiveness and the end of the exile. Again, Wright succinctly captures the meaning behind these actions:

> The Temple was the greatest Jewish symbol, and Jesus was challenging it, claiming authority over it, claiming for himself and his mission the central place the Temple had occupied. The Last Supper was Jesus' own alternative symbol, the kingdom-feast, the new-exodus feast. And, just as the Temple pointed to the sacrificial meeting of the covenant God and his people, the sign of forgiveness and hope, of God dwelling in their midst as the God of covenant renewal, covenant steadfastness, covenant love, so now Jesus by his double action was claiming that here, in his own work, in his own

person, all that the Temple had stood for was being summed up in a new and final way.[118]

Likewise, the Last Supper in the upper room was a symbolic action in which Jesus showed what the reign of God was like: a divine, eternal feast in which the liberated covenant people of God would celebrate the end of their exile from God. Again we look to Wright to describe how Jesus' actions functioned as symbolic prophecy:

> [Jesus was pointing to] actions of judgment and salvation that he believed YHWH was about to accomplish. In this context the words that he spoke suggest that Jesus was deliberately evoking the whole exodus-tradition and indicating that the hope of Israel would now come true in and through his own death. His death, he seems to be saying, must be seen within the context of the larger story of YHWH's redemption of Israel; more specifically, it would be the central and climatic moment toward which that story had been moving. Those who shared the meal with him were the people of the renewed covenant, the people who received "the forgiveness of sins," that is, the end of exile. Grouped around him, they constituted the true eschatological Israel.[119]

The true eschatological Israel would take up Jesus' subversive call. Remember that he has been proclaiming the presence of the reign of God; God's reign of justice and peace, stewardship and compassion; forgiveness for sinners, and hope for all the oppressed. In these actions, Jesus was rebellious and subversive of political power. He was subversive of the way in which the powers of the "old age" do business and subversive of all power that is based on the threat of death.[120]

In like fashion, then, the true eschatological Israel would not engage in armed revolt against the Roman state; and secondly, followers would overcome evil when it presented itself by turning the other cheek, or by going the extra mile.

Just so, Jesus would embody the task given to Israel: "He would turn the other cheek, he would go the second mile; he would take up the cross. He would be the light of the world, the salt of the earth. He would be Israel for the sake of Israel. He would defeat evil by letting it do its worst to him."[121]

He would be crucified.

Crucifixion: A Humiliating Death Penalty

Crucifixion was widespread in the ancient world, despite—or perhaps because of—its extreme cruelty. During the Maccabean period, Jews administered it even against other Jews as punishment for treason. Alexander Janneus, Hasmonean king of Judea from 103-76 B.C., ordered 800 Pharisees to be crucified for rebellion, an action for which the Pharisees gained revenge after his death by crucifying eighty Sadducees at Ashkelon. Crucifixions of Jews by Jews ended during the time of Herod; however it continued to be enforced against the people of Israel by other nations.

Roman crucifixion. The Romans who were living in Israel during the time of Jesus used crucifixion as a political and military punishment for persons in the lower classes, slaves, violent criminals, and rebels in the provinces. Sentences were carried out publicly so as to have the maximum effect as a deterrent. Flogging, and sometimes torture, often preceded a crucifixion.

Each culture in the ancient world developed its own variation on how crucifixion was to be carried out. Roman crucifixion began when the condemned person carried his own *patibulum* (cross-beam) to the place of his execution. Stakes or scaffolds were already erected at the spot. The *patibulum* was laid onto the ground, where its victim's arms were affixed to the beam with ropes or nails, sometimes both. Beam and body were then raised and fastened to the upright post or scaffold. A wooden block in the middle of the post supported the suspended body. Crosses were slightly higher than a person's height, unless its sufferer was to be held up for public display at a distance. The victim was sometimes drugged.

The cause of death by crucifixion is disputed, with some claiming that it came by asphyxiation when its victim's arms could no longer support his body. However, as the body was also supported at the person's crotch, the cause of death was most likely prolonged exposure, dehydration, and starvation. If a victim had been severely tortured or flogged, death could come from loss of blood or the nature of the wounds. But the point was that a person could be tortured for days "at relatively small expense."[122]

Throughout the crucifixion ordeal, the condemned person was often naked, utterly humiliated, subjected to ridicule, and often never buried— and lack of burial was the crowning horror in the ancient world. The whole spectacle of crucifixion satisfied a lust for revenge; it gave both rulers and executioners ample opportunity to exercise sadistic impulses.

Gospel Accounts of Jesus' Trial and Crucifixion

The *consistency* of the Gospel accounts of Jesus' preparation for arrest, his trial, and his crucifixion help us understand the Passion story from the perspective of its *relevance as a historical event*. All four Gospels discuss Jesus' going to the Garden of Gethsemane before he was arrested and crucified.[123] Prior to that occasion, the synoptic Gospels record relatively similar accounts of the planning related to Jesus' betrayal and death, and of the Last Supper.

The passion chronology. The consistency of detail surrounding Jesus' crucifixion gives historical credibility to the event. Let's review a few of the salient points.

- The story begins with Jesus and his disciples in Gethsemane; we recall the synoptic texts' portrayals of Jesus' prayer in the garden. At this point, Jesus could have avoided arrest; however, all four Gospels recount that this was the place of his capture.

- Jesus' trial before the Sanhedrin is reported in all three synoptic texts.

- Peter's denial of Jesus ("You are not one of his disciples, are you?" He denied it, saying, "I am not.") is common to all the Gospels.

- All the Gospels report that Jesus is delivered to Pilate, and they record that trial. Only Matthew talks about the death of Judas, and reports Pilate's wife's statement that Jesus is innocent. Only Luke and John recount Pilate's declaration that Jesus is innocent. Only Luke discusses Jesus' appearance before Herod. All the Gospels recount that Pilate forces a choice between Jesus and Bar Abbas; then Pilate sentences Jesus to be crucified. Matthew and Mark testify that Jesus was mocked by soldiers.

- All four Gospels describe the walk to Golgotha and the crucifixion. The synoptic texts identify Simon of Cyrene as the one who carries the *patibulum.* They also define "Golgotha" as having to do with the "skull."[124] All record the messianic inscription.

- On the cross, Luke records Jesus saying three "words": (1) on behalf of the Roman soldiers who are to be forgiven because they do not know what they are doing; (2) on behalf of one of the criminals who defends him, saying, "Today you will be with me in Paradise;" and (3) on his death, an outcry of *megale phonee,* or "loud voice," saying, "Father, into your hands I commit my spirit."

- During the execution John reports Jesus saying three "words": (1) commending his mother to the beloved disciple and the beloved disciple to his mother; (2) requesting something to drink in "I thirst,"[125] and (3) announcing his death with "It is finished."

- Matthew and Mark include only one "word." Jesus quotes Psalm 22:1, "My God, My God, why have you forsaken me?" The question for us is whether this is an act of pious recitation of the entire psalm, which ends in thanksgiving for deliverance and in hope, or whether this is a cry of anguish, a cry on which the first two-thirds of the psalm elaborates. Mark seems to favor the latter, because the *megale phonee* is used both in connection with the quotation from the psalm and at the time of death without any connection between them. Matthew might support the former interpretation because the *megale phonee* is connected with *palin* (again). Either way, it seems that Jesus died with a cry of anguish.

- Mark (15:44-45) and John (19:34) indicate surprise that Jesus was already dead. Matthew (27:51-53) and Mark (15:38) offer a midrash on Jesus' death with the rending of the temple veil and the resuscitation of the "saints."

- The three synoptic texts report the awe of the centurion.

None of these details seems unusual in terms of what is known of Roman crucifixions. They were justified as supremely effective deterrents against political and military crimes; to give up this form of execution was thought to potentially undermine the authority of the state. This means that Jesus' actions were consistent with scholarship describing the reasons for crucifixion. The details surrounding the event lend further historical credibility to the event.

The Cross in the Confession of Jesus' Disciples

Was Jesus crucified?

Early Christian proclamation and writing ascribes responsibility for Jesus' crucifixion to his Jewish enemies. Acts 2:23 says, "You crucified and killed [this man] by the hands of those outside the law." A chapter later, Acts 3:15, says, "You killed the Author of life, whom God raised from the dead."[126] Even more significant is Paul's use of a formula similar to the Acts texts in the earliest written document of the New Testament, 1 Thessalonians 2:14-15:

> For you, brothers and sisters, became imitators of the churches of God in Christ Jesus that are in Judea, for you suffered the same things from your own compatriots as they did from the Jews, who killed both the Lord Jesus and the prophets, and drove us out; they displease God and oppose everyone.

A contrary argument would point to a rabbinic interpretation of Deuteronomy 21:22-23 which played a significant role in the Jewish *rejection* of crucifixion as a form of the Jewish death penalty, at least from the beginning of direct Roman rule. The passage reads:

> When someone is convicted of a crime punishable by death and is executed, and you hang him on a tree, his corpse must not remain all night upon the tree; you shall bury him that same day, for anyone hung on a tree is under God's curse. You must not defile the land that the Lord your God is giving you for possession.

While some might say that the Deuteronomic text could have diminished the probability that Jesus was crucified at the instigation and insistence of Jewish authorities, the historical evidence cited throughout this chapter is too strong to cast any serious doubt. The important question is that this text made it impossible for Jews to think of someone who had been crucified *as Messiah*. Hengel reminds us that "(t)he cross never became a symbol of Jewish suffering. . . . A crucified messiah could not be accepted either."[127]

The cross as integral to Jesus' messianic mission. Jesus died as the crucified Messiah, and thus, his death had and has to do with his messianic mission—that is, with his being "savior." The Gospel of Mark reports the essential nature of the cross to his mission. In Mark 8:31-33, he seeks to teach this to the disciples:

> Then he began to teach them that the Son of Man must undergo great suffering, and be rejected by the elders, the chief priests, and the scribes, and be killed, and after three days rise again. He said all this quite openly. And Peter took him aside and began to rebuke him. But turning and looking at his disciples, he rebuked Peter and said, "Get behind me, Satan! For you are setting your mind not on divine things but on human things."

Likewise, Mark 9:30-32 and Mark 10:32-34 show Jesus' repeated attempts at discussing the events that would unfold—but in each of the texts they do not understand.

The very idea of the cross was initially an offense—that is, the thought that the Son of God was revealed through crucifixion was utter madness, and, further, the expectation that someone ought to believe such a story suggested that the speaker thought little of the listener's intellectual capacity.

However, Paul insists that in the event of the cross God is reconciling not just Israel, but the whole world. The steadfastness of his conviction does not mean his proclamation was accepted without reservation or suspicion. Indeed, his twenty-two-year ministry often "reaped no more than mockery and bitter rejection with his message of the Lord Jesus who had died a criminal's death on the tree of shame."[128] And yet he persisted. Indeed, his letter to the Galatians also cites the same Deuteronomic text. He writes, "Christ redeemed us from the curse of the law by becoming a curse for us—for it is written, 'Cursed is everyone who hangs on a tree.'"[129] Understood rightly, this text corresponds with his assertion that the Father gives up the Son "for all of us" (Romans 4:25 and 8:32), and the Son accepts a slave's death in obedience (Philippians 2:7-8).

In Romans 4:25 (He was "put to death for our sins and raised for your justification"), Paul places Jesus' death in relation to our past: He died for it. And it places Jesus' resurrection in relation to our future: He rose for it. Our past life is forgiven; our future life is justified. In fact, his resurrection gave the world a future that is beyond the mere absolution of its guilty past.

This interpretation of Jesus' payment for our guilty past, however, is still inconsistent with the larger message of what God is doing in Jesus. The crucifixion is not Jesus' act of sacrificing himself so that the Father can be merciful. Here it is important to say that the crucifixion was not a vicarious satisfaction of divine honor (understood as justice or wrath, and so on). As Gerhard O. Forde points out:

> Put in its most crass form, this view would hold that Jesus' death is a sacrifice in which he is a substitute for us who pays

the divine justice what is due for human sin and/or appeases the divine wrath. . . . There seems to be a virtual consensus among contemporary biblical scholars, however, that this tradition finds little support in the Scriptures, either in the Old or New Testament. Scripture never speaks of God as one who has to be satisfied or propitiated before being merciful or forgiving.[130]

Forde's assessment is that Jesus dies because God *insists* on being merciful. This view is consistent with Jesus' messianic mission. The point for us is that as the Jewish rejection of Jesus as *crucified* Messiah intensifies, so does the confession of Jesus as the crucified *Messiah*—or, as Tillich observed—the crucifixion of Jesus was an event which became a symbol. The resurrection of Jesus was a symbol which became an event.

Atonement in the History of Theology

The most famous quotation on christology is Philipp Melanchthon's brief word in the *Loci Communes,* "This is to know Christ (namely), to know his benefits."[131]

A contentious history. Let me begin this section by citing a couple of quotations that are important for our understanding of the works of Christ as they pertain to atonement. First, referring to Melanchthon's quote above, Hultgren says:

> In the same paragraph Melanchthon goes on to say, over against the scholastic theologians, that knowing Christ is not a matter of perceiving "his natures and the mode of his incarnation." Nor is knowing Christ achieved by an acquaintance with the historical or earthly Jesus. One can know Christ only in light of his redemptive work: "Unless one knows why Christ took upon himself human flesh and was crucified, what advantage would accrue from having learned his life's history?"[132]

And then Forde has these comments:

> If he is raised by God and thus attested to be Lord and Christ, then a death and life antithesis between our idea of

divinity and God's appears in him. Had he remained in the tomb we would have been right. Since he has been raised he is vindicated and we are wrong. That is the end of us. All of which is to say that successful movement in Christology from a language of substance to the language of act can be made only when it drives to a proclamation that does the act of God *to* us. Christ cannot merely be talked about; he must finally be *done to* us. Christ has been explained to us endlessly, dressed and redressed in everybody's clothes, painted in everybody's color and likeness, fashioned and refashioned into everybody's hero. The explanations never seem to stick. If he is to be our Lord and Christ he must finally be proclaimed so as to *do us in* and make us new.[133]

Finally, Hans-Joachim Iwand, who is quoted in Moltmann's *Crucified God*, begins his remarks on the cross by pointing out that it "is the utterly incommensurable factor in the revelation of Christ. We have become far too used to it."[134] Now, let me insert just a comment here on Iwand's thought. It is significant that the church of the first four centuries never used a cross as a visual symbol. Of course not! Christians were still being crucified. So the cross didn't become jewelry until the Middle Ages, and now it's a chic piece of adornment because it's so symmetrical. One just has to remember this. Instead of a cross, early Christians used other visual symbolism: Jesus as shepherd was popular on tombstones and elsewhere. And of course, the fish symbol. But not the cross! At least not as long as the Romans were still doing it to the Christians!

Iwand continues:

> We have surrounded the scandal of the cross with roses. We have made a theory of salvation out of it. But that is not the cross. That is not the bleakness inherent in it, placed in it by God. Hegel defined the cross: "God is dead"—and he no doubt rightly saw that here we are faced by the night of the real, ultimate and inexplicable absence of God, and that before the "Word of the cross" we are dependent upon the

principle *sola fide*; dependent upon it as nowhere else. Here we have not the *opera Dei,* which point to him as the eternal creator, and to his wisdom. Here the faith in creation, the source of all paganism, breaks down. Here this whole philosophy and wisdom is abandoned to folly. Here God is non-God. Here is the triumph of death, the enemy, the non-church, the lawless state, the blasphemer, the soldiers. Here Satan triumphs over God. Our faith begins at the point where atheists suppose that it must be at an end. Our faith begins with the bleakness and power which is the night of the cross, abandonment, temptation and doubt about everything that exists! Our faith must be born where it is abandoned by all tangible reality; it must be born of nothingness, it must taste this nothingness and be given it to taste in a way that no philosophy of nihilism can imagine.[135]

And this is the scandal of the cross: that our faith in Christ begins where Jesus is abandoned—by humankind, certainly, and apparently also by his God. The importance of experiencing and confessing the death of Jesus as saving—that is, as atonement—can hardly be exaggerated. One of the epochal books on this subject is *Christus Victor.* It would be difficult to discuss the Christian Gospel in the twentieth century without some reference to Gustaf Aulén's work in this book, and we will pay attention to it here.

The subject of the atonement is absolutely central in Christian theology. Each and every interpretation of the atonement—and here we will briefly look at three—is more closely connected with some conception of the essential meaning of Christianity, and, therefore, reflects some conception of the divine nature. Moreover, the history of the doctrine of the atonement is such an important a part of the history of Christian thought in general that the judgment which is formed on *this* part of the history, on its conflicts and its changes, must largely determine the judgment which is formed as to the meanings of Christian history in general.

First we must take up the topic of interpretations of the death of Jesus on the cross advanced through the course of Christian history. Aulén writes:

My work on the history of Christian doctrine has led me to an ever-deepening conviction that the traditional account of the history of the idea of the Atonement is in need of thorough revision. The subject has, indeed, received a large share of attention at the hands of theologians; yet it has been in many important respects seriously misinterpreted. It is in the hope of making some contribution to this urgently needed revision that this work has been undertaken.[136]

The revision which Aulén then undertakes is that we cannot start a history of the idea of the atonement by beginning in the Middle Ages with Anselm's *Cur Deus Homo* (why God became human), but that's been the tradition. That is, Anselm's work has had an inordinate influence and impact on western Christian theology. It is the doctrine of the salvation of God in both Catholic and Protestant scholasticism. It is the foundation of quintessential conservative American Protestantism. It is the four spiritual laws. It is D. James Kennedy's evangelism explosion. It is still the most popular notion, and you will recognize it immediately when we start laying it out.

But Aulén says we can't begin with Anselm; we must start with the ancient church: with Irenaeus and Anthanasias and Gregory of Nyssa and others. With this background, he tries to identify theological motifs, or approaches, to atonement theory (we could almost call his work "models" of atonement), and he suggests three types:

- Classic: Jesus is champion and victor.
- Latin (or objective): Jesus is substitute.
- Subjective: Jesus is example.

The classic type: Jesus is champion and victor. In this approach to the atonement we say that Christ has freed all persons whose lives were in bondage (to sin, death, and the devil), and he freed them by defeating the powers that kept them enslaved. The metaphor is the battlefield, and Jesus is God's champion.[137] A sixth-century hymn, "Welcome, Happy Morning," is an example; its first verse is:

"Welcome happy morning!" age to age shall say;
"Hell today is vanquished, heav'n is won today!"
Christ, once dead, is living, God forevermore!
Him, their true creator, all his works adore.
"Welcome, happy morning!" age to age shall say.[138]

Hell is vanquished: defeated! And heaven is won! The background for this approach comes straight from Irenaeus (130-200). He wrote that humankind "had been created by God" that we might have life. "If now, having lost life, and having been harmed by the serpent," were humankind "not to return to life, but were to be wholly abandoned to death, then God would have been defeated. . . ."[139] Again, notice the battlefield language here; the use of "defeat" points to its alternative—victory.

Reflecting on Matthew 12:29,[140] Irenaeus continues, saying, "and the malice of the serpent would have overcome God's will. But since God is both invincible and magnanimous, [God] showed [God's] magnanimity in correcting [humankind], and in proving all [people], as we have said; but through the Second Man [God] bound the strong one, and . . . annihilated death, bringing life to [humankind] who had become subject to death. For Adam had become the devil's possession, and the devil held him under his power, by having wrongfully practiced deceit upon him, and by the offer of immortality made him subject to death. . . ." This is one of Irenaeus's favorite explanations for human sinfulness: that humanity had succumbed to the deceit of Satan: "God was really trying to keep you from being God." It's a misinterpretation of Genesis 3, the text that says, "eat the fruit of the tree and be like God, because you will know the difference between good and evil." Satan's characterization of the consequences was partly true; but he partly misconstrues God instructions, and so in the end Satan is deceitful. John 8:44 takes up this lie by pointing to the devil that was the father of lies, for he lies from the beginning.[141]

So here we get to the point Irenaeus is making: "For by promising that they should be as gods, which did not lie in his power, he worked death in them. Wherefore he who had taken man captive was himself taken captive by God, and man who had been taken captive was set free from the bondage of condemnation."[142]

Now Iranaeus is an example of very early thinking in the church, and he is one of the first theologians for whom we have a fairly complete theological statement. About 100 years later we have Athanasius (298-373 A.D.), writing in *The Incarnation of the Word of God*, "Thus it happened that two opposite marvels took place at once: the death of all was consummated in the Lord's body; yet, because the Word was in it, death and corruption were in the same act utterly abolished."[143]

And along similar lines, Gregory of Nyssa (330-395 A.D.) develops the same idea further with:

> What would [the devil] accept in exchange for the thing which he held, but something, to be sure, higher and better, in the way of ransom, that thus, by receiving a gain in the exchange, he might foster the more his own special passion of pride? . . . The Deity was hidden under the veil of our nature, that so, as with ravenous fish, the hook of the Deity might be gulped down along with the bait of flesh; and thus, life being introduced into the house of death, and left shining in darkness, that which is diametrically opposed to light and life might vanish; for it is not in the nature of darkness to remain when light is present, or of death to exist when life is active.[144]

Notice that what Gregory says is that because the bait was the flesh of the *Logos*, it's indigestible.

A fair amount of biblical support for the use of battlefield language exists.[145] The framework is dualistic: two powers contending. Aulén qualifies "dualism" so that it doesn't mean there is an absolute power of good, which is God, and an absolute power of evil, which is Satan. Here "dualism" means that God's rule meets with resistance and that when resistance is undone, then there is reconciliation or atonement, God's reign undisputed. But in the classical theologians, whose approach to atonement is being discussed here, it is clear that the devil had rights over fallen humanity; the leading purpose of the cross was to satisfy those claims.

Gregory of Nyssa also asserts that God beats the devil at his own game: deceit. Was God practicing deceit on the devil in Jesus being the *Logos* incarnate as the bait on the hook? Gregory says something like, "Yes, but the devil deserved it!" Gregory is saying that because the devil is deceiver from the beginning, it is quite appropriate that the one who deceives is also then the one who is deceived.

In this dualism, the anti-godly powers—Satan, death, sin, and wrath—enslave humans. Sin is viewed as bondage in this model. "The devil made me do it" is a way of mocking the powers that resist God. Living with an addiction is taking seriously the powers that resist God.

But Jesus is the divine champion who battles the powers, conquers them, and liberates humanity. The change takes place in our situation, in our circumstance, in human history. We were in bondage; now we are free. We were enslaved; we are liberated. The powers that enslave—whether they are ideologies, addictions, or death itself—are ultimately powerless.

This "classic" theory of the atonement is not without its problems. Most important to notice is that it does not understand the depth of what happens to and in God. It also makes spectators of the redeemed, for we are hardly held accountable for our sins. We don't really need forgiveness; we simply need to be rescued, like damsels in distress. And who can blame the damsel, the victim, for being in distress? Although the theme of human bondage is timely, the imagery is passive and does not allow us to understand the approach experientially in our contemporary lives.

Moreover, we hardly have to attend to this cosmic battle since Christ will win it regardless. Our only response is to sit in the cheering section. Neither are we required to *do* anything. We have no motive for change in behavior; thus this approach contains insufficient basis for Christian ethics.

The Latin type: Jesus is substitute. The Latin type became ascendant in the Middle Ages, its rise dating from *Cur Deus Homo* (*why God became human*) by Anselm of Canterbury (1033-1109). This treatise is the best known and most widespread interpretation of the atonement in the Christian West. Two hymns provide examples. The first verse of "Ah, Holy Jesus" is one:

Ah, holy Jesus, how hast thou offended
That man to judge thee hath in hate pretended?
By foes derided, by thine own rejected,
O most afflicted.[146]

Another example, this one contemporary, is the chorus of "Lord, I Lift Your Name on High":

You came from heaven to earth, to show the way
From the earth to the cross, my debt to pay
From the cross to the grave, from the grave to the sky
Lord I lift your name on high. . . . [147]

What Jesus does here is not defeat our enemies but pay our debt, take our punishment. Anselm writes:

Just so inexcusable is man, who has voluntarily brought upon himself a debt which he cannot pay, and by his own fault disables himself, so that he can neither escape his previous obligation not to sin, nor pay the debt which he has incurred by sin. . . . If the two complete natures [divine and human] are said to be joined somehow, in such a way that one may be Divine while the other is human, and yet that which is God not be the same with that which is man, it is impossible for both to do the work necessary to be accomplished. For the Divine will not do it, because he has no debt to pay; and man will not do it, because he cannot. Therefore, in order that the God-man may perform this, it is necessary that the same being should be perfect God and perfect man, in order to make this atonement.[148]

Biblical passages supporting the Latin approach abound.[149] Mark 10:45 and Matthew 20:28 are referred to as the *lutron*, ransom, passages: "For the Son of Man came not to be served, but to serve, and to give his life as a ransom for many." Notice here that the ransom has no object. The text does not say give a ransom to the Father, and yet this supposition that God demands payment is at the heart of Anselm's theory.

Hultgren points out that nowhere in the New Testament is the death of Jesus ever something offered to the Father. Not ever! This means the biblical basis for this approach is shaky.

At the same time, ransom passages such as John 1: 29 ("The next day he saw Jesus coming toward him and declared, 'Here is the Lamb of God who takes away the sin of the world!'") raises the question of meaning of the sacrificial system in the Old Testament. Is the sacrifice offered *to* God, or is it offered *by* God *to* Israel? You see, with this correction, the sacrificial system is not so much directed to God as gift *from* God.

Sacrifice also assumes culpability, so the language here uses the metaphor of the courtroom. A product of Anselm's time, the framework is feudal law, with debts and obligations, and the possibility of substitution. It assumes a feudal lord who keeps order and who works justice. The infractions of God's law are ours, but Jesus pays our debt. Only then can reconciliation be reached.

In feudal law people were members in a social hierarchy. If you were a peasant, you were required to give so many days of work to the Lord of the manor on which your lands existed. The rest of the time you were allowed to devote to the care of your own land and your crops. Similarly, if you were a knight under service to a Lord you were obligated to give to that Lord the traditional forty days of service in a year—not many days, but you could also pay for a substitute to fulfill your service. If you didn't perform your duty or find a substitute, the Lord could extract a payment from you.

Now Anselm adapted this elaborate feudal system to saying something like, "Ah, that's the way God deals with sin—except that the penalty for sin is infinite, and therefore, we can't pay it off."

This approach depends on the theory that God's justice demands satisfaction (compensation) for infractions of the divine law. Sin is infraction; it is "breaking the law." The penalty is eternal death, damnation

(Romans 6:23: "The wages of sin is death"). Since all humans are guilty (1 John 3:4: "Everyone who commits sin is guilty of lawlessness"), each human being's life is already forfeited, and hence no person's death can save neither himself, herself, nor others.

Now remember that we said above that feudal law permits a substitute to step in to pay the fine or take the punishment. Here we can rely on Tertullian's teaching about merit to allow Jesus' righteousness as satisfaction for the sins of the whole world. God's demand for justice would be met by Jesus' perfect life and innocent death. Because Jesus is the God-man, Jesus can offer a sacrifice which has *substitutionary* quality. That is, as a human being, Jesus can replace other human beings; and because Jesus is infinite God, his replacing another human being has infinite value. Thus, Jesus alone can make satisfaction for all human sin.

Moreover, because Jesus' life was without guilt (active obedience), his vicarious death (passive obedience) at the hand of sinners preserves God from being the executioner. Jesus' passive obedience to both divine and human authority shows the perfection of the sacrifice made to God to satisfy the system of "justice" which Anselm assumes. Since God's justice is satisfied, God can now be merciful to sinners without violating the demands of justice. This means that *the change takes place in God;* namely, the Father's need for satisfaction is satisfied.

Proponents of the Latin approach to atonement begin with Anselm of Canterbury who seeks an answer to the question of why God became human. For example, if God could just zap the powers and principalities, why was the cross necessary? Scholastic theologians, both Catholic and Protestant, were even more severe than Anselm. Jesus' death became the chief element in Christianity because "the cross saves"; as such, Good Friday eclipsed Easter and Christmas.

This approach, too, has its problems. First, it reduces sin to immorality. Notwithstanding the passive nature of Jesus' obedience, in fact, God the Father is the executioner of God the Son, thereby separating God's justice from God's love. It also misreads the biblical witness by purporting that the Son dies to placate the Father.

The Latin type also provides an inadequate basis for Christian mission and ethics because it gives human beings little to do besides be sorry for causing Jesus' death and be grateful for their redemption. Part of the problem here is that neither Catholicism nor scholastic Protestantism offers a basis for the Christian ethic. This carried forward into modern Evangelical atonement theology; when you die, you tell God the right answer ("Jesus died for me as punishment for my sin, so now you can let me into heaven"). But this theology also has no basis for ethics. As a result, Evangelicals must start over again with another requirement, and say something like, "Now, in order to be *qualified* while you are still alive, you must accept Jesus as your Lord and Savior." Then, once you do that, there's nothing more to be done to live a Christian life. Some Evangelicals have seen the pitfalls of this and so want ethical constraints to "prove your faith." But it's too late! You're already in heaven! The angels have rejoiced by now already! The orchestra is playing! God is satisfied! And you know very well that you don't have to do anything more. (This is like the old Lutheran pastor who, on his deathbed, assured his family that he was certainly going to heaven because he couldn't think of having done a single good work!)

The subjective type: Jesus is example. Unlike the two types above in which God does something and achieves reconciliation for us "out there"—where we are not active participants, this metaphor for the Atonement is subjective and is based on images from the classroom. Its aim is not defeating the powers or satisfying the law, but rather, it seeks our transformation. The nineteenth and twentieth centuries are replete with examples from Christian piety. The hymn, "Lord, Speak to Us, that We May Speak," is an example. The first verse is:

> Lord, speak to us, that we may speak
> In living echoes of your tone;
> As you have sought, so let us seek
> Your straying children, lost and lone.[150]

The language reflects the pietist tradition. Its theme is, unquestionably, "Jesus is our example." This idea of example, or learning a lesson, also can be seen in the work of Peter Abelard (1079-1142). He wrote:

Now it seems to us that we have been justified by the blood of Christ and reconciled to God in this way: through this unique act of grace manifest to us—in that his Son has taken upon himself our nature and persevered therein in *teaching* us by word and example even unto death—he has more fully bound us to himself by love; with the result that our hearts would be enkindled by such a gift of divine grace, and true charity should not now shrink from enduring anything for him.[151]

So on being properly taught and learning our lessons, we are then to be transformed by Jesus' example. Now, while some point to John 13:15 ("For I have set you an example, that you also should do as I have done to you") or 1 Peter 2:21 ("For to this you have been called, because Christ also suffered for you, leaving you an example, so that you should follow in his steps"), neither of these biblical texts really support the "Christ-as-example" approach as support for the work of atonement between God and humanity.

Still, this approach continues to attract its followers. The educational framework instructs followers to think of God as a teacher who shows people, primarily, how to love. Humankind can be better at being one with God and God's creation if effectively taught. The challenge is merely a matter of God finding the right audio-visual aid. As those go, the cross is an impressive example of explaining just how to "lay down one's life for one's friends."[152]

Likewise, problems abound with this approach. Jesus has no need to be divine; he is merely valedictorian in a class that includes other holy people, from Socrates to Gandhi. As for human sin, it is viewed as ignorance or weakness. People just don't know what is expected, and can't seem to learn what God has been trying to teach. Humans fear God—but without reason, for God is love. Because of this fear, humans are not free to love God or each other. This means that if people could just understand that there is no need to fear God or the neighbor, if humankind could just live from a changed heart, reconciliation would be realized.

The most significant problem with this approach is its shallow understanding of sin. People are regarded as a little dull-minded, but not really sinful, rebellious, or in bondage to sin. An absence of any concept of "the wrath of God" prevails throughout its message. Love is, therefore, reduced to sentimentality; recall examples such as the television program, *Touched by an Angel*,[153] or the film, *It's a Wonderful Life*.[154]

This approach also emphasizes that Jesus reveals that "God is love" through his life and especially through his death on the cross—understanding which surely is expected to cause people to experience a breakthrough in learning about God's love. When God loves people "this much," comprehending this love is not only a revelation; it also is an attitude all persons would want to emulate. Jesus becomes an example not only of God's love for humankind, but also of humankind's love for God and of humankind's love for one another. Followers want to be like Jesus, to follow his example, to love and forgive and work for justice and live for the kingdom. The goal of Jesus' example is for individuals to change their minds (subjective) about God and thus follow Jesus. *The change takes place in us.*

In addition to Abelhard, proponents of the subjective approach to atonement include Schleiermacher, Albrecht Ritschl, plus followers of liberal Protestantism and Protestant pietism.

Christians have plenty to do—but "example" is considered an inadequate basis for Christian ethics. In reaction to the neo-orthodoxy of the nineteenth century and twentieth century, this approach is generally out of favor.

Summary of three theories of atonement. Aulén's three theories of atonement help us recognize the truth of our experience when Holy Week lays guilt on us for causing the Son of God to die, when Easter is a shout of victory, when week after week we are exhorted to see what God has done or what Jesus has done and go forth to do the same. The "models" go in and out of favor in the church, and as individuals we will favor one or another.

However, even though Aulén holds up the first model as more biblical, we must note that some aspects of each of the models are grounded in the New Testament. An element of truth supports each one. We also should take note of Forde's words: "Theories do not reconcile. If dogmatics covers the offense [of the cross] with its theories, it cannot serve a proclamation that actually *is* a ministry of reconciliation."[155]

An alternative approach to atonement. The inadequacies of the three ways of talking about atonement require us to find a fourth way. We already have the foundation for this in our discussions in the previous chapter. The first part of that foundation is the proclamation that Jesus Christ is raised from the dead, his life vindicated, and his death obliterated by God.

This obliteration of Jesus' death leads to the second part of the foundation: Jesus is God, the long-awaited Messiah who reconciled the people to God after a seemingly interminable exile. This entirely Jewish concept of return and restoration from exile is not good news only for the people of Israel, however. The good news is for the whole world.

The surprise for everyone was the way that Jesus, the Messiah, ended the exile. It was not through military might, nor through religious ritual or purity. This Messiah reconciled humanity and God by suffering at the hands of those whom God loves, and at once exposing the impotence of their power and the depth of God's forgiveness and mercy. This revelation necessitated a radical reinterpretation of what "Messiah" meant to Jesus' Jewish disciples.

A Reinterpretation of "Messiah"

The disciples' proclamation of Jesus as crucified messiah used and broke all concepts which made it intelligible in the ancient world. It used and broke the concept of Messiah from the Old Testament by understanding messiahship radically new in the light of Isaiah 53. Crucifying the Messiah—that's not supposed to happen. But when we understand the Messiah in light of the Suffering Servant—now we have a new insight into God's promise.

The event of the cross also used and broke all Hellenistic concepts of vicarious and saving death—for one's city, nation, or the truth—for Jesus' death was God's death, and it was for the entire world! That is, it was not just for one's friends, but also for one's enemies! The Greeks might ask, "Even the Barbarians?"

Finally, the event of the cross used and broke the concept of temple sacrifice in both Jewish and Gentile religion. Jesus is the end of cultic sacrifice whether given by God or offered to God. Here we think of Hebrews 13:10-16, which includes, "Therefore, Jesus also suffered outside the city gate in order to sanctify the people by his own blood. . . . Through him, then, let us continually offer a sacrifice of praise to God, that is, the fruit of lips that confess his name." Doing good here arises out of what God already has done and is doing in the cross and redemption of the creation.

The cross of Jesus happens to God. The event of the cross is an act of redemption which God enacts. First, God initiates and offers atonement through the cross. We see this most clearly in 2 Corinthians 5:19, in which Paul writes, "In Christ, God was reconciling the world to himself, not counting their trespasses against them, and entrusting the message of reconciliation to us." God does this work. Redemption may be *proclaimed* by the church, but God *does* it. And when Jesus announces that sins are forgiven in his name, he is then saying that through him, God accomplishes the saving act of restoring the relationship between God and people.

Secondly, God identifies with our sin. The Father gives up the son, as we see in Romans 8:32 ("He who did not withhold his own Son, but gave him up for all of us, will he not with him also give us everything else?"); but the Son gives himself into death for us, as in Galatians 1:4 (which refers to Christ as the One "who gave himself for our sins to set us free from the present evil age, according to the will of our God and Father").[156] Thus, the alienation of sin happens to both Father and Son (Mark 15:34). God takes our sin into God's existence (2 Corinthians 5:21); it is a sin which expresses itself as the generational alienation and the guilt of parents and children. When the sinless one is made to be sin, God's "perfection" (or to say it another way, God's deity) is revealed as compassion. You see, God's deity is beyond morality; it is now compassion: *compassio* means "suffering with."

We recall Luther's assertion that "God is here dealing with God," in that God overcomes God's own wrath (Romans 1:18ff). Through the event of the cross, God participates in an act of giving up and being given up. Through Jesus, God participates in the experience of alienation, sin, and death. And finally, as forgiver, God overcomes sin by enduring it, by taking it into God's very being and history. You see, in forgiveness, the forgiver does not retaliate; the forgiver does not even the score. The forgiver absorbs what is done.

The cross of Jesus happens to the world. The world—that is, all of humanity—crucified the Messiah. By all of humanity, we mean religion and politics; Jew and Gentile; enemies and disciples; men, women, children—you name it, everyone is responsible for the crucifixion. No one is exempt. This means Jesus' death calls the whole world into question. Jesus is, in some sense, vindicated in the resurrection. But the *unmasking* of false gods takes place in the very act of dying. As Helmut Gollwitzer says, "Pilate and Herod are revealed."[157] They are revealed as persons who won't take anything seriously or are willing to crucify the Messiah in order to save their own skins—and Gollwitzer was quite pointed about his message. His book, *The Dying and Living Lord,* is a series of sermons he preached in 1940 in Berlin—with the Gestapo in the congregation. When he preached his sermons on the crucified Christ during Lent, he was arrested. They took him on Palm Sunday to cut off his preaching.

Likewise, the world is revealed as "old aeon." In the death of Jesus, the world's oldness—its way of death-dealing in order to cling to the illusion of life, its way of making victims in order to cling to the illusion of power—is revealed. That is, the old has passed away; it has come to an end.[158]

In the death of Jesus, God has made a final and irrevocable decision about the world. God will not abandon the world. God will not give up on the world. Atonement means that the world has been changed by God's identification with it in the depth of its oldness.

The cross of Jesus happens to humankind. The event of the cross is transforming. It changes us. Forde says, "[T]he cross occurred so that it could happen to us in our present."[159] That is, God is concerned with the creation in the here-and-now. This is why Jesus' death makes our death and life possible: Jesus dies in our place—that is, in the place where we die. We do die! One to a customer! So Jesus dies not "instead of us, but ahead of us."[160]

Faith in Jesus, then, means death to sin instead of death in sin. It means freedom to give up false objects of trust, false gods, false ways of dealing with our sins. Jesus, thus, is the grounding in God, in history, and in us for our dying to sin and rising to newness of life.[161] Romans 6:1-11 is instructive here, especially verses 9 to 11:

> We know that Christ, being raised from the dead, will never die again; death no longer has dominion over him. The death he died, he died to sin, once for all; but the life he lives, he lives to God. So you also must consider yourselves dead to sin and alive to God in Christ Jesus.

From Crucifixion to Resurrection

In this chapter we have articulated important convictions about christology. Three bear reasserting here: First, on the basis of the resurrection of Jesus, the disciples of Jesus experienced Jesus as the eschatological Messiah, the final judge, and therefore in some real sense "God." Their earliest devotions (prayer, worship, hymnody) are directed to Jesus as if they are directed to God. Their earliest titles are high titles; even Paul most probably ascribes the title "God" to Jesus.[162]

Secondly, this divinity is not in antithesis to the life and activity and death of Jesus. It is *about* the life and activity and death of Jesus. Hence, the death of Jesus on the cross is something that in some real sense happens to God. And third, this means that if the confession of Jesus, the Christ, as God has its starting point in Jesus' resurrection from death, the Christian confession of the Triune God must have as its starting point Jesus' death on the cross.

To discuss the confession of the true God authentically, that is, as the Triune God, we need to address two closely related topics:

- Jesus' death on the cross happens to God and is a saving event. But, we might ask, what does it *mean* that God suffers, and that God dies? Can such language have any significance for us? This will be addressed in Chapter 6.

- The Holy Spirit is the eschatological Spirit of God's salvation. We will cover this topic in Chapter 7.

Before we move on to these two topics, we need to discuss the resurrection of Jesus as the power of the future. This is the subject of our next chapter.

In the Trinity Term of 1929 I gave in, and admitted that God was God, and knelt and prayed: perhaps, that night, the most dejected and reluctant convert in all England. I did not then see what is now the most shining and obvious thing: the Divine humility which will accept a convert even on such terms. The Prodigal Son at least walked home on his own feet. But who can duly adore that Love which will open the high gates to a prodigal who is brought in kicking, struggling, resentful, and darting his eyes in every direction for a chance of escape? . . . The words *compelle intrare*, compel them to come in, have been so abused by wicked men that we shudder at them; but properly understood, they plumb the depth of the Divine mercy. The hardness of God is kinder than the softness of men, and His compulsion is our liberation.

C.S. Lewis, Surprised by Joy

CHAPTER 5

THE RESURRECTION OF JESUS AS THE POWER OF THE FUTURE

The meaning of the resurrection of Jesus includes the confession that he is the final power of the future. This confession determines what it means to live in the present. It means that there is more to do with life than to preserve it. For if Jesus is the final power of the future, then the way we "believe in Jesus" is to experience the freedom of the Spirit to offer our lives into the service of the reign of God.

The claim that Jesus is the final power of the future also determines the meaning of the term "salvation." Jesus is not only the Lord of the outcome of history in a general sense. The church also confesses that he, quite specifically, is the Coming One. The Nicene Creed confesses, "He will come again in glory to *judge* the living and the dead, and his kingdom will have no end." The Creed concludes, "We look for the resurrection of the dead, and the life of the world to come."

Eschatology has traditionally dealt with the meaning of creedal statements by discussing the outcome of history; the visible end of "this (old) age"; and the visible consummation of the reign of God, the final judgment, the death and resurrection of all humanity, and the eternal destiny of humanity—that is, eschatology has dealt with "heaven" and "hell." These so-called "last things" usually have been discussed at the end of dogmatic and systematic theology. However, I am not waiting to the end to take up these "last things"—although I used to do that. Over the years, I have come to see that this topic, despite its subject, fits more appropriately here, after I have made the claim that Jesus of Nazareth, identified as the Christ by his resurrection, is the standard by which all theological work is to be shaped. Now I'm going to try to carry out that claim as radically as I can.

The task. If by his resurrection Jesus has been identified as the Christ, the second person of the Trinity, then we must re-envision the future: We must think differently what the future means. And once we do that, we must retrieve the past differently. As such, we will move in two time directions out of the proleptic center of the resurrection of Jesus. For prolepsis means you look at the future differently—or you experience it differently. Or you see the outcome in the midst of things.

Past, Present, and Future

For human beings, the future can be the occasion for anxiety and dread. We may experience it advancing toward us, unknowable and unstoppable, minute by minute, second by second, hour by hour. We cannot escape it. It is inexorable. Likewise, the past: We cannot undo it. We experience its presence in memory and in records. Here we are looking at history going in two directions at the same time.

In *The Structure of Awareness,*[163] Thomas C. Oden addresses an issue on this topic, which was most brilliantly raised by Tillich. Tillich was trying to say that the questions, the issues, that had been raised for theology varied in accordance with the three great periods of Western intellectual history in which they took place. The great question in classical antiquity, Tillich said, was the question of being and non-being: Will we be? Will we not be? This was a question for the immortality of the soul, the kind of thing that is discussed in the Socratic dialogues about which Plato writes.

Next, the Middle Ages paid attention to the question of guilt. Here the Lutheran Reformation is, in a sense, the climax of attention to the question of guilt. Finally, the question for the present, Tillich says, is meaninglessness: Today we are struck by the importance of meaning.

Oden says that while there is some justification for saying that a dominant issue is associated with a particular age, it is more accurate to say that these are questions for each of us in terms of different time dimensions of our own existence. The question of *guilt* is the appropriate response for dealing with one's past. The question of *being* is appropriate for dealing with one's future, and the question of *meaning* is the appropriate issue for dealing with one's present.

How we deal with guilt and being and meaning vary, but Oden lays out a scheme to think about them. He says our access to the past is through memory, and this means that through memory our past reveals our guilt: Should we have done the things that we did not do? Should we not have done the things that we did do? Should we have done some better or differently. Questions of guilt arise with what has, in fact, occurred—or at least as we remember them occurring. Our response, or at least the most common response, is to justify what we have done: "Why, no! We wouldn't do a single thing differently!" Or, "We'd do it all again, exactly the same way." Or, "We did the best we could!" Or, "If you had been in our shoes, you would have done the same sort of thing!" If we engage in any self-doubt in this context, it is usually to rationalize our actions: that we cannot be held accountable. If we are unable either to justify ourselves or to avoid accountability, we dread that accountability will render us inappropriate, useless, worthless human beings. The point is that most of us continue to drag our pasts along with us; we keep seeking better ways of coming up with rationalizations that will allow us to cover our actions, and make us less culpable, less guilty.

The second period is the present, and here access to events is through the immediacy of our experience. The predicament that it produces is boredom—and don't all of you now nod! The problem of meaninglessness in the present is that it leads us to look for distractions: *anything* to relieve the tedium or monotony of the moment! Television is almost made for this kind of response.[164]

The third period Oden addresses is the future, and on this topic we gain access through our imaginations. What can we anticipate? For what do we look? The predicament we face with this journey into the unknown is anxiety. Will *this* happen? Will *that* happen? Will my hopes be realized? Will my fears be realized? The response we generally give as a way of coming to terms with this uncertainty is some variation of denial, or despair, or worry. Contingency, ambiguity, and indeterminateness compel us to live with illusion or fatalism. We are threatened by this unknown—both because of what we do *not* know (the *un*certainty of its possibilities), and because of what we *do* know (the *certainty* of death). We cannot escape either one.

We bear witness to the threatening character of both past and future by the ways in which we falsify the past *and* falsify the future. But Jesus grounds and alters the experience of the future—and that is the topic I am taking up here.

Undoing the future as progress. First we want to say that it is the inexorability—that is, the inevitability—of the future that provides the occasion for unfaithful responses. One unfaithful response would be the tendency to substitute optimism for Christian hope. For example, the optimistic Enlightenment belief in "history" as "progress" has proven to be both ambivalent and dangerous.[165] By "progress" we mean that we now accept as a "given" that as we move from period to period in history, from age to age, from decade to decade, almost from year to year, we are guaranteed that things will be better than they have been in the past. True, some things have improved: It is quite clear today that we have both medical techniques and medication to make childbirth a) safer, and b) less painful. My daughter-in-law illustrates this. First, they were able to induce labor; secondly, they had everything monitored. My wife said the number of cords and machines was incredible; they could tell blood pressure instantly! Heart beat instantly! The medical professionals could read this information in both my daughter-in-law and the baby! And when they induced labor, they were able to give pain medication that enabled my daughter-in-law to participate in the delivery while not enduring some of the sharp pain that's often associated with childbirth. I compare this to when I was a child; we always said a prayer of thanksgiving after a birth to express gratitude that God had preserved the life of the mother in her *peril* and in her pain. We in the developed world hardly think of peril any longer in connection with delivering a new baby, but in the nineteenth century, women died regularly and routinely in childbirth. It was not a foregone conclusion that you would survive.

Likewise, we remember that before the Civil War, surgical operations, if there were any, were performed without anesthesia. You got a shot of hard liquor and you got something to bite down on before a doctor sawed away on your bones: That's where we were 150 years ago. So today we are—medically and in many other ways—better off than our ancestors were.

However, in the midst of these wonderful advances, we do not recognize (and this is why the current notion of progress is a dangerous notion) that not everything that changes—and even not all of the things that seem to be beneficial—are without a whole new set of problems which we were not able to anticipate. This is one of the things about which ecologists are continually speaking. The WorldWatch Institute in Washington, D.C. reports an alarming prognosis for our planet, precisely because of many of the things we have done to make our lives most comfortable. The Institute gives us perhaps forty to fifty years to reverse some of the dimensions of our own lifestyles, and say that the consequence for ignoring a turnaround will be that within 200 years the planet will be uninhabitable by most of our descendants. And the people at WorldWatch are not alarmists.[166] They do not just go out on a limb for a few causes; they are trying to take a look at the general state of the world.

The economy also provides examples. One of the difficulties for developing nations is the lack of enough resources for everyone on this planet to live the kind of life we have in a Switzerland, a Sweden, a Canada or the United States. Just not enough. The gap between the rich and the poor grows greater each year.

So what I'm saying here is that progress can be thought of as something similar to the ramp/cane syndrome: You adjust the curbs at street crossings so that people in wheelchairs can negotiate their way across the intersections—only to create a virtually impossible situation for people who are blind and need to use their canes to find curbs so they can navigate dangerous crossroads. You solve one problem only to create another. The analogy I'm making is that the concept of progress needs to be challenged radically. What we cannot do is simply say, "Time makes things better." That is, we cannot optimistically claim that just moving on into the future means somehow things are going to improve for everyone.

The importance of truth about the past. We also cannot claim that we can "make up" the past (as if to say, "Oh, I'll make it up to you . . ."), or forget the past, or escape the past. Neither can we ignore the implications that past actions may have on future events. Destructive futures result from the violence of tyranny, oppression, abuse, and reaction. Here I'm thinking of the contrast made by Hannah Arendt in her book, *On Revolution.*[167] She points out that as revisionists look at the American Revolution, they are saying, "Well! The argument between the U.S. and England wasn't all that great. I mean, the injustices were often fairly minor and trumped up. England was a very benign imperial power in fact." Therefore, the reaction to England was neither profound nor characterized by a great deal of violence.

By way of contrast, however, the French Revolution of the same period was a response to abuses which were real—and often enormous. And the reaction was horrendous! When prisons were stormed, people who were incarcerated were murdered wholesale! These crimes could not be ignored, even in the name of "revolution."

In recent decades, we remember the reactions in African countries liberated from truly oppressive colonial rule. Think of the 1960 massacres of Belgian citizens in the land that formerly was the Belgian Congo [now the Democratic Republic of the Congo]. Evil in the past can have implications for the future, and we cannot simply look the other way when tyranny and oppression are being imposed upon peoples.

Events such as these are senseless, so we try to make sense of them within their contexts. We seek meaning in history. Sometimes we ask why God allows horrible events to occur. We ask questions such as "What did God intend by . . . ?" We ask one another what lessons are to be learned. I keep thinking, for example, of all the commentaries that were written when John F. Kennedy was assassinated in 1963: Everybody was trying to find some lesson in a dreadful event—trying to take some meaning from it, to mitigate and to modify the horror of what had happened. People were trying to discern some sort of divine plan and purpose in the midst of what seemed to everyone to be a quite senseless act.

In fact, they were asking about God: How could God allow this assassination to happen? They were defending God's goodness in the midst of chaos—as if God needed defending.

Grabbing all the gusto. The threatening character of the future often leads to denial of time or denial of mortality. We think of Woody Allen's jokes: "I'm not afraid of death. I just don't want to be around when it happens," he says.

Or we deny that we are aging. We take the "feel-young" laxative, and use Grecian Formula to darken gray hair. We pretend that we are perpetually young and that aging is not happening to us. The images of our culture are not images of aging. A few years ago, Schlitz Beer tried a commercial with the slogan, "You only go around once in life. You've got to grab all the gusto you can." The tape showed an aging deep sea diver handing on his gear and his skills to his son. The father grabbed his gusto. Now it's the son's turn. They sold zero beer with that commercial. Why? Nobody thought of having had their gusto and passing on the opportunity to somebody else. You want to keep grabbing your gusto for as long as you can! That's the whole point!

When we realize our denials don't work, when our tyrannical attitudes cannot be ignored or forgotten, when the threatening character of the future is more than we can bear, the only thing left is despair. Despair is the absence of hope. It is a feeling of the absurdity of life. As Edna St. Vincent Millay said, "It is not true that life is one damn thing after another—it's the same damn thing over and over."[168]

Now in the face of these various false interpretations about the future, Christianity claims this: Jesus is the power of the future.

Altering Expectations of the Future

Jesus grounds and alters the experience of the future. When we see what God is doing in and through Jesus, we gain new insights. Why do we need these insights?

Kant thought that the religious concepts of "God," "freedom of the will," and "eternity" (together with something like the "immortality of the soul") were necessary for human morality. He said that this world and our life expectancy in it are not enough to address injustice and to balance the books. On the one hand, we need a kind of cosmic book-balancer—a divine judge (which was Kant's understanding of God). With this concept of God, we need freedom to make choices so we can be held accountable. We also need eternity to balance the books, so that you will get yours at some point, even if you don't get it in this life—and I'll get mine, too, of course, which we each assume is going to be to our own advantage!

These concepts, said Kant, could not be "known" phenomenologically—that is, directly through tangible or visible experience. We cannot know freedom or eternity because there is no sensory data available for them. Not even descriptions of so-called "near-death" experiences contribute sensory knowledge to ideas of "God" and "eternity"—because they are exactly what they are called: *near*-death! Those who describe them are not yet, and have not been, dead! Symptoms of oxygen deprivation to the brain may occur, or perhaps some other phenomenon we don't yet understand because of the difficulty of replicating it in a laboratory. Whatever it is that is being described, it is *not* a description of what happens to the dead, or they would not be here telling us about it.

It was distressing in a sense to see Elizabeth Kübler-Ross, who helped so many of us come to terms with people who were dying and to deal with their losses as honestly and as sympathetically as we could, to clutch at near-death experiences as if they were some evidence that there truly is a) God, and b) immortality. These experiences are not beyond death; they are still on this side of it. There is no way to *know* from *near*-death what might be on the other side. Only one who is *beyond* death can ground the expectation of the final or the eschatological future. That is why, in Christianity at least, everything depends upon and must be determined by the event of Jesus as the Christ. Only one who is beyond death can ground the expectation of the final or eschatological future. It is the Christian claim and confession that Jesus is the one who is beyond death. *He alone* is, therefore, the grounding for all Christian expectation of the final or eschatological future. He also determines the character of that expectation. In Jesus, the Christ, the expectation can be *known*.

I am struck here by Paul's letter to the Ephesians, because it is the example of either colossal faith or colossal insanity. He writes:

> I pray that the God of our Lord Jesus Christ, the Father of glory, may give you a spirit of wisdom and revelation as you come to know him, so that, with the eyes of your heart enlightened, you may know what is the hope to which he has called you, what are the riches of his glorious inheritance among the saints.[169]

Notice here that Paul says that there was *knowledge* to be gained from the encounter with Christ who is the Risen One. The future in Christ is not something which unfolds and "develops"—not something which is "there," just in the normal progression of time as we creep from one day to the next, arriving at the petty pace that Shakespeare talks about as he writes, ". . . for which we wait, which fills us with anxiety or dread, whose fulfillments are transient and capable of disappointment." Even when you achieve your so-called goal, whatever is achieved is a transient goal. You may even be disappointed that what you had been looking for does not turn out as you had imagined. In contrast, Paul is talking about knowledge of something that is already true, already real, already fabulous: a rich and glorious inheritance. That is why we confess that Jesus is the Coming One. To proclaim that he is the Coming One means that he comes to us from the future and is therefore the only authentic ground of hope. That is, he comes *at* us. Here we can look to Moltmann, who says it is interesting that both the German and the Latin terms describing this phenomenon have a different character to them. The German word is *Zukunft*, meaning future—and has as one of its major components, "*Zu*"—that is, it is not *we* who are coming to it, but *it is coming* to us. *It is advancing* upon us. It is *engaging* us from the *future*. Or the Latin: *ad-ventus*—"*ad*," again: to come toward; "*ventus*," coming. "*Ad-ventus*" then refers to that which is *coming toward* us, which is *advancing* to meet us: That's the kind of image we must have.

Moltmann points out that the future for which we wait will itself pass away, for future as "what will be" will itself become "what has been." That is, the future of today also will go out of *existence* if it is only whatever we come to in the normal process of going through minutes and hours and days and months: When you get there, it's over, it's gone. I have a photograph of the Sunday afternoon visit to hold my grandson, but the *moment* is over; it is past, and it does not exist anymore. There is only the memory and a photograph.

But the future of Jesus, the Christ, means "the end of becoming and the end of passing away."[170] He is saying that what comes to us in Jesus is not transient, disappointing, or disappointable. It will not pass away. It means the end of "becoming" altogether.

Envisioning the future. The future in Christ inaugurates already here and now the reign of God and its ultimate consummation when the powers of "this age"—including sin and death, transiency and disappointment—are visibly disclosed to be subject to the Messiah (1 Corinthians 15:24-28). That is, they have no power because of Jesus the Christ. The inbreaking of the reign of God is a proleptic vision of the outcome of history in the midst of history.

We might want to try to identify what the vision of the reign of God is. If one looks, for example, at the imagery of the prophets, starting particularly with Isaiah, we see an image of harmony in all of nature, when the lion will lie down with the lamb. The vision of the prophet of Isaiah is that the child can play with the most dangerous of beasts because there will be no danger any longer. The time is one of universal peace and of universal justice.

Or we could look at the studies of the fiftieth year—the so-called jubilee year. The jubilee year means the forgiveness of all debts and the return of all property to its original owners. Some sources say that we do not know that this was ever done in Israel; it would be economically catastrophic to do anything like that. But the mere thought of it sent lenders scurrying; they wouldn't lend money the last couple of years before the fiftieth year because they were afraid somebody just might invoke the jubilee year. When Jesus says in the synagogue in Nazareth, "Today this scripture is fulfilled in your hearing," they want to throw him over a cliff! They don't want to hear that! It was a dangerous thing to say—but it is the vision of the reign of God. It is the vision of final justice—the justice that the "haves" do not want and the "have-nots" do.

The point we are making is that Christian hope is grounded in Jesus, the crucified Christ, whose offering of himself breaks the power of death, because death cannot render the offering meaningless. Instead, in the resurrection, it is *death* that loses its former meaning as "the end of hope." Christian hope is, therefore, in the triumph of life over death, the triumph of the Spirit of God over the spirit of the demonic.

Jesus Is the Object of Trust for Christian Life and Hope

Trust/hope in Jesus as the final power of the future means a radical change in our participation in history. I am intentionally referring to trust/hope with a slash between them—and here's why: When Thomas Aquinas talks about the theological virtues, faith, love, and hope are the three great virtues. At the time of the Reformation, one of the difficulties theologians faced was that persons of the papal party and persons of the Lutheran party were not able to understand each other. At least part of the reason was that Luther understood "faith" to mean what Aquinas meant with regard to "hope"—that is, entrusting of oneself to the God of the future. One outcome was that when Luther said justification is by faith alone, his opponents thought he was *eliminating* hope and love, and instead, referring only to an intellectual activity. That is precisely the opposite of what Luther was trying to do. So to be clear, I write trust and hope with a slash between them—as trust/hope—as a way of trying to say, "This is what we are talking about, the concepts together as one. It is, in a sense, what you do when you let go of the trapeze bar and commit yourself in mid-air to whoever is going to catch you. That's what Luther means by faith. So trust/hope is the final power of the future.

Trust/hope, then, means liberation from the bondage of self-projection. It means the "edenic" (that is, Eden-like) freedom of unthreatened and unthreatenable vulnerability and selfhood.[171] It means the freedom for compassionate availability and mutual servanthood: These are the ways you entrust yourself to Jesus.

Creaturehood. Trust in Jesus means acceptance of our creaturehood and, hence, acceptance of our finitude. The great problem is that we are not content to be what we are. Tillich points out that the fall into sin is the alienation of our true selves, or our authentic selves, so that the fall is not something that happens in ancient times with ancient people. "Fall" is the experience of that alienation of the truth about myself.

Similarly German theologian Helmut Thielicke talks about the "divided self"—that is, he refers to the misconception of "body" as a shell which houses the "real self," the "soul."[172] His book *Death and Life* takes place during the Third Reich in Nazi Germany. At that time, he was one of the scholars under *Schreibverbot:* literally, the prohibition of writing or publishing anything. To further limit his influence, the authorities exiled Thielicke to a parish in Wittenberg and forbade him from taking along his theological library. So banished to a parish, in the middle of the Second World War, he wrote this important book—without any of his resources, forged out of the memory of his own recalled learning. He nonetheless accomplished marvelously analytical work in which he discusses how we have denied our own creaturehood by means of a false concept which he calls the "divided self." The concept was not invented by Thielicke, but he names it and explains that those who hold to this misunderstanding think of the body as merely a shell which houses the *real* self (the soul) and, further, believe that the soul is indestructible, that as soul, the *real* "me" will live forever.

Similarly, Harold Bloom discusses the American consciousness and says that this sense of the *real* "me" may well be as old as God. He points to Gnostic ideas claiming that the *real* "me" is an indestructible self which can be separated from the mere transitory, physical, historical, bodily existence that I have now.[173] And that fallacy, says Thielicke, is running from the kind of creature that we are.

In truth, the issue is that we *are* souls—not that we *have* souls, but that we *are*. What does this mean? In Genesis, God breathes into this earth-creature that has been fashioned from the dust of the ground, and the earth-creature *becomes* a living soul—this is precisely the language which is used!

Bibically, the concept "soul" refers to a dimension, not a component of human being. We *are* "souls." That is, we have unique relationship with and accountability to God. Think of it this way: "I," "me," "this being" stand in many kinds of relationships: I am a child to my parents, a grandchild to my grandparents, a husband to my wife, a father to my three sons. I am teacher to all of you. I am citizen of the U.S.A. and of Columbus, Ohio. This idea of "me" isn't my left arm. All of me is citizen; all of me is husband; all of me is father: Those relationships are dimensions of my existence. The word "soul" is such a dimension. You will not find soul by dissecting me on an operating table, as you will find my liver and my lungs, because the soul is *me*, all of me in relationship to God who is the object of my trust and my hope and my life.

Because we are sinners, death is more than biological. It is evaluative, the judgment of God upon the "alienated self." Biology is the vehicle for that more profound, uniquely human experience of death. In his *Spoon River Anthology*, a book of gravestone mini-biographies, Edgar Lee Masters discusses one that features a carving that is supposed to be a dove. But, says Masters, it looks like a chicken! Then, his character muses that we all are like chickens, except that we can see the ax from the first—that is, we are aware of our mortality in a way that other creatures are not.

Franklin Jones

If I could have lived another year
I could have finished my flying machine,
And become rich and famous.
Hence it is fitting the workman
Who tried to chisel a dove for me
Made it look more like a chicken.
For what is it all but being hatched,
And running about the yard,
To the day of the block?
Save that a man has an angel's brain,
And sees the ax from the first!

Therefore, we spend our lives anticipating it.[174] That we can see the ax from the first makes death more than biological. We experience our *lives* as being evaluated. Perhaps we suspect that the world can get along without us: That's an evaluation. Such an appraisal does not mean good or bad; it just means dispensable. And we are, in fact, dispensable. Dreadfully dispensable! I would like to think that I am important to a few people, but I know that another professor will take this place the moment I am not here. So the point I am making is that, as creatures, we understand that life and death are intertwined. And how we experience ourselves as creatures informs how we experience our relationship with God.

Continuity and discontinuity. To accept our creaturehood, our finitude, also means that we await the resurrection of the dead. Death involves the whole person. It is, quite literally, the end of our possibilities—but death is not the end of God's promise and eschatological power. For in the resurrection of Jesus, God is *beyond death*. "Death no longer has dominion over him" (Romans 6:9).

Jesus' resurrection is not self-vindication for Jesus. He is the first fruits (1 Corinthians 15:23), the "firstborn of all creation" (Colossians 1:15). This means it is not for his sake that he is raised from the dead—but for ours! The fact that death does not have dominion over him is for our sake. Hence, Christians confess the resurrection of the body rather than the immortality of the "soul" (1 Corinthians 15:53-57). Paul said this mortal body must put on immortality; it does not inhere. That is, mortality is not inherent in immortality; it is not a characteristic or quality of immortality. This cannot be stressed sufficiently enough.[175]

When we await the resurrection of the dead, we are aware that the structure of the resurrection is new creation, in which there will be both continuity and discontinuity (1 Corinthians 15:36-49). This is what Jesus means in the Gospel of John when he says, "[U]nless a grain of wheat falls into the earth and dies, it remains just a single grain; but if it dies, it bears much fruit." Hence, there is continuity with what is planted, but also discontinuity because it is new creation.

The Meaning of Salvation

Salvation means the coming (already begun in the mission and resurrection of Jesus) and ultimate (not yet, still awaited) consummation of the reign of God, the purpose and goal of God in history. To be saved is to share in the enterprise which is the reign of God. This is what Jesus is saying in Matthew 25 when he points out that "we will find him nowhere but in the brokenness of the world—in the last, the lost, the least, the little, and the dead."[176]

The topic of salvation must be dealt with in terms of Jesus, the Messiah, as having the final power of the future. He is identified as Savior—nothing else. This means that if he is called Judge, it is judge as Savior. The point to be made here is simply this—that above all else, Jesus is "Savior."

The reign of God, of which Jesus is "alpha and omega," inaugurator and consummator, encompasses all nations, all creation. For in the outcome, or "eschaton," God will be "all in all" or (in another translation) "everything to everyone" (1 Corinthians 15:28). He cannot be defeated by anything—not death, not sin, not satan.

Perspectives on salvation. Christian theology has a history of speaking of salvation as the alternative to damnation, of speaking of the destiny of individuals in terms of "going to heaven" or "going to hell," and speaking of "evangelism" as that aspect of the church's mission which involves preaching Jesus as Savior to persons who are unevangelized so that they can accept him as Savior and thus be admitted to heaven instead of being eternally condemned to hell. In his book, *No Other Name*, John Sanders describes a spectrum of perspectives on "the destiny of the unevangelized." Sanders is evangelical, and the foreword to his book is by Clark Pinnock, who once taught at Trinity Evangelical Divinity School in Deerfield, Illinois—one of the six very conservative divinity schools. These are not thinkers who are trying to evade certain uncomfortable teachings.

Sanders identifies two extremes: restrictivism and universalism. By his definition, restrictivism means that all the unevangelized are damned eternally—that God predestines to damn some people to their damnation, according to John Calvin. Similarly, Augustine wrote that beginning with Pentecost, those who have not received Christian baptism are damned.

By universalism, Sanders means that all are saved no matter what they believe. Persons who agree with this position would be Origen, nineteenth-century Boston clergyman Charles Chauncy, and twentieth-century Anglican bishop John A. T. Robinson.

But Sanders does not stop there. He then identifies three positions that he calls "the wider hope":

- inclusivism,
- universal evangelization, and
- eschatological evangelization.

Inclusivism refers to the idea that salvation is universally accessible also apart from Christ, even if people are unaware that salvation comes through Christ. Proponents include Charles Wesley, C. S. Lewis, and Pinnock.

Universal evangelization before death says that all persons are somehow evangelized before they die in ways of which we are not aware. Thomas Aquinas apparently held this position.

Finally, eschatological evangelization claims that our destinies are not necessarily determined at death. In the final outcome, however, all persons, whether evangelized in this life or that which is to come, will confess Jesus as the Christ and author of our salvation. Paul says every tongue will confess and every knee will bow (Philippians 2:6-11). While Hans Schwarz raises arguments against this position, referring to it as a "universal homecoming,"[177] it supported by Carl Braaten, Gabriel Fackre, Robert Jenson, and George Lindbeck, among many others.

It is important to stress that eschatological evangelization (also called universal salvation)—which is my own view—is not the same as "universalism." I am saying that Jesus alone is the Christ and that all will finally participate in God's eschatological salvation because finally all will confess him to be the Christ. This view lives with the conviction that death cannot defeat God's will for the world, and, therefore, we trust in the hope that all will confess Jesus as the Christ and share in the eschatological salvation of the reign of God.

For Christian life in the present, what we do know and believe matters because it tells us how we should live *now*. Evangelism is the job of *all* Christians because it is the mission of Jesus. Braaten and others put this as strongly as possible, saying that the reign of God has come, and it is appropriate—indeed, necessary—for the church to call people into its service. Evangelization belongs necessarily to the mission of the church because all are to be called to participate in witness and service to the reign of God as grounded and consummated in Jesus the Christ alone.

Universal*ism*, on the other hand, asserts that all paths to salvation—via whatever religion one opts into—are valid and lead one to "God." For a professed Christian to espouse this belies a misunderstanding of the Trinity, for underlying it is the assumption that Jesus is not *quite* the same as "God," but just one of God's several "special children."

Which is it? We will not know more in this life. We may never know more.

Heaven and Hell

Among the most misunderstood and misapplied concepts in Christian theology are concepts of heaven and of hell. Here we will look at some of the predominant views and, finally, consider the authority of the Bible and the thoughts of a few eminent scholars.

The concept of heaven. In the pre-Copernican worldview, "heaven" was understood to be a "place" high above the earth to which one's soul could "go" after death or where the "saved" person would reside after the resurrection from the dead. In contrast, "hell" was regarded as a "place" far under the earth where the damned would experience eternal torment. Elements of such a worldview can be found in New Testament writings, particularly the ascension narratives.[178]

Martin Luther identified "heaven" with the creedal and Biblical phrase, "the right hand of God," which he takes from Psalm 98:1: "O sing to the Lord a new song, for he has done marvelous things. His right hand and his holy arm have gotten him victory." For Luther, the "right hand" is where God is gaining the victory through the saving event of Jesus as the Christ. By this he means that wherever the Gospel is gaining victories, there is heaven, there is the right hand of God. In many ways, this is how the Jews substituted the word "heaven" for the name of God (which is ineffable), so that the Kingdom of Heaven does not mean a place outside this world, but is simply a way of not using the tetragrammaton YHWH. To say it another way, they would replace YHWH with "heaven" in referring to the reign of God.

C. S. Lewis, in *The Great Divorce*, pictures "heaven" as reality itself, and "hell" as too small to have any substance. "All Hell is smaller than one pebble of your earthly world; but it is smaller than one atom of *this* world, the Real World," he says. "Bad cannot succeed even in being bad as truly as good is good. . . . Only the Greatest of all can make Himself small enough to enter Hell."[179]

He also talks about how people become real. He says we start out as shadows, unable to walk on real grass: It hurts one's feet until one becomes "real." So heaven is not ethereal; it is final reality.

Finally, we benefit from paying attention to Robert Jenson, in "How the World Lost Its Story":

> If, in the *post*-modern world, a congregation wants to be "relevant," its assemblies must be unabashedly events of shared apocalyptic vision. "Going to church" must be a journey to the place where we will behold our destiny, where we will see what is to come of us. Modernity's version of Christianity—that is, Protestantism—has been shy of vision and apocalypse alike. Just so, its day is over.
>
> Preaching and teaching and hymns and prayers and processions and sacramental texts must no longer be shy about describing just what the gospel promises, what the Lord has in store. Will the City's streets be paved with gold? Modernity's preaching and teaching—even its hymnody and sacramental texts—hastened to say, "Well no, not really." And having said that, it had no more to say.

The truly necessary qualification is not that the City's streets will not be paved with real gold, but that gold as we know it is not real gold, such as the City will be paved with. What is the matter with gold anyway? Will goldsmiths who gain the Kingdom have nothing to do there? To say with this one little piece of the vision, our discourse must learn again to revel in the beauty and flexibility and integrity of gold, of the City's true gold, and to say exactly why the world the risen Jesus will make must of course be golden, must be and will be beautiful and flexible and integral as is no earthly city. And so on and on.

In summary, "Heaven" must be the subject of the church's exuberant apocalyptic language (e.g., Revelation), recognizing that the destiny which is the gift of the Risen Christ is more real than our present experience of reality, more concrete, more beautiful, more just, more joyous, more full—not less. Here, because it is grounded in Christ, our imagination is free to be boundless.[180]

The concept of "hell." The Jewish *sheol* as "abode" of the dead is a neutral concept, not a place of punishment. Its counterpart is the Greco-Roman *hades*, also a neutral place to which all the dead go.

It is possible that Jesus made references to the "hell of fire" (from the Greek: *gehenna to puros)* in referring to the valley of Hinnom where child-sacrifice and cremation once took place.[181] We might think of it as something like the garbage dump of Jerusalem. Elsewhere, the story of Lazareth and the Rich Man does not use the word hell at all; it, too, uses the word *hades*.[182]

As a place of punishment, the idea of hell enters Jewish thought during the persecutions of Antiochus Epiphanes in the second century B.C., originating perhaps from Persia, and it becomes an "apocalyptic" concept. As such, it is more related to violent deliverance breaking into history from the outside than it is to the eschatological perspective of the Gospel.

Outside of Matthew and some Markan parallels, only James and 2 Peter refer to "hell." Nobody else does.

Despite the references to "hell" ascribed to Jesus, there is no grounding for the concept in what happened to Jesus as the crucified and risen Messiah. How shall we imagine it without any grounding? Some quotations are instructive here. First, in Romans 4:16-17, Paul writes:

> For this reason it depends on faith, in order that the promise may rest on grace and be guaranteed to all his [Abraham's] descendants, not only to the adherents of the law but also to those who share the faith of Abraham (for he is the father of all of us, as it is written, "I have made you the father of many nations")—in the presence of the God in whom he believed, who gives life to the dead and calls into existence the things that do not exist.

Next, Robert Jenson on "The Last Judgment," writes:

> If there is to be a universal community of righteousness, as Jesus' resurrection promises, then between its perdurance [duration] and the perdurance of our present community of unrighteousness something must happen. . . . The biblical promise of final "judgment" . . . refers to the move from the history of unrighteousness to the history of righteousness.

> Judgment is the act which restores the community to its right life, done by one who can do it. Cf. Genesis 16:5; Exodus 18:13-16; Isaiah 11:1-9. . . . The last judgment will be the one after which another is not needed. Which is to say, it will be that one in which God answers the prayer to "Rise up, O Lord, and judge the earth yourself."

> Biblically, then, judgment is thus a matter of putting the community to rights. It is not primarily a matter of rewarding or punishing individuals according to some general measure of deserts, but of putting individuals into the communal places in which they can meet others in mutual care. . . . In the final

judgment God will accomplish truly and permanently what penultimate judgments brokenly and temporarily accomplish. The final judgment will not be the separating of the sheep from the goats (we must always remember that Jesus' parable *is* a parable), but the putting of God's universal creation to rights. This need not mean "universal salvation." What if there should be one who persisted eternally in his/her refusal to be in one community with the rest of us? What will Himmler do, confronted with all those Jews who will be determined to love him?

What is new about the final judgment in the New Testament is the identification of the final judge: Jesus, the Christ. He is the head of the church, that is, of that human society destined to be universal. The final judgment will be the universal insertion of God's people into the righteous life of the Father with Jesus the Son in the Spirit. It will be our subjection to appropriate places in *that* community.

Will any be left out? That would mean to be left outside of God. Where would that "outside" be? Supposing Himmler refuses to be loved by Jews, where will he go to avoid them? And indeed, supposing there were someplace to go and he went there, would not that be to *evade* judgment? To evade the debunking (of our boasting), the exposure (of our lovelessness), the awe (involved in beholding the Father) which insertion into the Triune life must be? The question between particularism and universalism is backwards to what is commonly thought. To ask, "Will God finally reject anyone?" is precisely *not* to ask "Will God truly judge the wicked?" It is to ask, "Will God let any escape his judgment?" That is, escape him?

Perhaps. Who knows? God is certainly free to let some flee eternally to a place outside himself, if even he can figure out what such a place would be. I confess I can neither figure that out, nor, if it is a possibility, see why God would let anyone hide out there. But there is much I do not understand."[183]

And then, Karl Barth said, "A person must be crazy to teach universalism, but impious not to believe it.[184]

Finally, Capon, in *The Foolishness of Preaching,* writes:

> The church's job is . . . to invite us all to go moonstruck over the news that the one operative consideration in our life is the *Passion of the Finder to find*—the wild enthusiasm of the God who makes all things, old and new, by bringing them out of nothing but *nothing.*

> Out of nothing, *Ex nihilo.* Out of 100 percent, 24-karat nonexistence. Not out of nothing as *precondition* of being, but nothing as the *matrix* of being from start to finish. One of the worst things that ever happened to the church was the importation into its doctrinal structure of the Greek notion of the immortality of the human soul. Because . . . it persuaded us that nothingness is something that God has no serious use for anymore. . . . We convinced ourselves that *we would never have to be nothing again.* Which gave us a mere half-reason for needing Jesus as our resurrection: We would never be more than half dead.

> When I urge people to chuck the immortality of the soul as a piece of anti-Gospel baggage, they worry. They tell me, "Look this is 1997. What about 2097? If I don't have an immortal soul, and the Rapture doesn't happen in the meantime, where will I be then?" I tell them, "*You* look. . . . You were nothing in 1797, and it hasn't bothered you so far. Why should it bother you now? Can't God do the same trick a second time?" . . . Jesus came to raise the dead. Not to repair the repairable, correct the correctable, or improve the improvable. Just to raise the dead, and nobody but the dead. . . .

> (That means that the only condition for our salvation is that we are dead!) If you like, you may refuse to believe that

you've been drawn into the eternal party. You can't stop the party, though. You may try, if you like, to walk out on it and look for another bar to drown your sorrows in. But it's the loneliest walk in the universe: there is no other bar, and when you get done with all your walking, you'll find you went nowhere. Jesus does seem to insist that we're capable of being stupid enough to try and stay in that hell forever—and that God will even go so far as to utter a frustrated Lover's "Oh, damn!" over our stupidity. . . . Yet even if it's the Gospel truth, all of your hell will be at the party, sequestered in the nail print in the left hand of the Bridegroom at the Supper of the Lamb.[185]

Clearly, the fear of "going to hell" is not the basis for evangelization. The Christian basis for evangelization is the liberating vision of the reign of God, which *does not comfort and set free* from the power of death and sin *without repentance and conversion.* To be grasped by and to live in that vision is the mission and joy of the church.

God is not in heaven; he is hanging on the cross. Love is not an otherworldly, intruding, self-asserting power—and to meditate on the cross can mean to take leave of that dream. . . . No heaven can rectify Auschwitz. But God who is not a greater Pharaoh has justified himself: in sharing the suffering, in sharing the death on the cross.

Dorothee Söelle, *Suffering*[186]

CHAPTER 6

THE SUFFERING OF GOD

Does God suffer?

How are we to think about this question? At one end, we might consider ancient Greek ideas about the qualities defining a deity. A god would be a perfect being whose attributes would reveal a divine personage without need: constant, invulnerable, and above (and therefore unaffected or unmoved by) affliction in the material world.

By contrast, a Christian perspective begins with the truth that Jesus is God. Since Jesus died on a cross, this view would allow that God suffers. To suffer is to be vulnerable—which also means that God is moved by the needs of the creation and, so moved, would be open to change.

Ronald Goetz calls the suffering of God "a new orthodoxy." He said, "Indeed, despite all the real and intractable differences among theologians, a curious new consensus has arisen. The age-old dogma that God is impassible and immutable, incapable of suffering, is for many no longer tenable."[187]

Goetz lists four reasons why the idea of the suffering of God makes sense today. The first is the decline in Christendom. If Christendom arose with Constantine (272-337 A.D.),[188] and reached its high point in the development of European Christianity following the period of Gregory the Great (ending after the year 604 A.D.), then one would have to ask, when did its decline begin? When did the advance of Christianity around the globe wane?

I would say the decline began with the rise of the Enlightenment, probably in the seventeenth century, and if you want to press the point, it might be connected to the religious wars of that time. We had begun to recognize that more than one tradition could exist in a particular political entity. England settled for multiple religions after the restoration of the monarchy in 1660; Germany resigned itself to it with the Peace of Westphalia in 1648; and in the new colonies which became the United States a plurality of faiths became a matter of principle—the concept even rose as a matter of Constitution in 1789. So these events signal the breakup of Christendom.[189] The results of this change in the separation of religious and political entities is now quite visible in the twentieth century, for God no longer is envisioned as victorious and triumphant in a conquering world in which Christianity prevails alongside, if not completely identified with, political powers.

The second reason put forth by Goetz—and the one that surprised me the most—is the rise of democratic aspirations. We define freedom and choice as the ability to alter our circumstances. In this context, we will not bow to a God who is immutable (unwavering) or impassible (unaffected by human suffering). We can take this notion further and say that since impassibility is an attribute emblematic of an imperious rule indifferent to its effect on those who are governed, then God must be resisted as a tyrant! So Goetz is saying that because immutability and impassibility were more characteristic of divine-right monarchy (where in a sense the governed be damned—subjects of the monarch just submitted, obeyed, accepted whatever circumstances came along), then democratic aspirations altered understandings of God.

Next he points to the problem of suffering and evil. Here I think of both world wars as examples of senseless suffering which raised anew the problem of evil. Tillich was a German chaplain during WWI, and he had a nervous breakdown because he found it impossible to have to bury young men, to have to deal with those who survived, to have to send the letters home to the parents. The whole enterprise was so utterly senseless! The generals were using tactics of battle devised for slow-loading muskets with very bad accuracy; with such weaponry, a charge into opposing fire had some hope of working. But what do you do when the guns are repeaters, when the machine gun has been invented and is in use; where a charge of men across an open field into defensive positions has practically no hope of any success, where they would measure how long you would live in terms of your rank: Privates would last three weeks, non-commissioned officers would last maybe five weeks, lieutenants would last two months, and so on. They wore belt buckles saying *Gott mit uns,* God with us—and they came to curse those buckles, because no evidence showed that God was with anybody. It was absolutely dreadful! Generals refused to go to the front because they couldn't order men into battle if they knew what was actually going to happen to them. It is necessary for us sometimes just to read histories of these wars to discover how they unleashed a wave of senselessness about existence and of cynicism about political institutions. Almost unanswerable questions for religion also were raised, for those were questions addressed to God.

Finally, Goetz's fourth reason dovetails with recent scholarly reappraisal of the Bible. The biblical portrait of God is "personal, passionate, jealous, concerned, and suffering." As such, we cannot portray God as an impassible and immutable deity. A passage such as "Jesus Christ is the same, yesterday, today and forever" does not mean that God is immutable; it means that God is utterly trustworthy—that's what Hebrews 13:8 is trying to say. To be trustworthy, to be reliable or dependable, does not mean that one is unchanging.

Goetz is saying that we must re-envision a suffering God at least in part through our own experience with the presence of God in the world. The old idea of the victorious, conquering God is set aside. Comparisons to human monarchs are likewise irrelevant. At the same time, awareness about the rise of evil throughout the creation demands a religious response. And the response which makes sense to us is the biblical portrait of God—the One who hangs on a cross, and who, as we will see, is a Triune God.

The task. In this chapter we will discuss how the freedom of God points to a God who suffers. These insights arise out of twentieth-century experiences that open us up to the presence of God in the midst of incredible evil in the world. We need to explore the depths of some of these experiences, as they allow us to delve into God's great desire to be with and for the creation in the midst of immense suffering.

God's Presence in the Midst of Human Suffering

To the four points being made by Goetz at the beginning of this chapter, I would add that a concern for the Jewishness of the God of the Bible as well as a recovery of the Jewish matrix of Christianity have contributed mightily to an emphasis on the suffering of God. A powerful example is recorded in Elie Wiesel's book, *Night*, in which he describes an especially horrific execution in 1944 in the concentration camp at Auschwitz where he was incarcerated:

> One day when we came back from work, we saw three gallows rearing up in the assembly place, three black crows. Roll call. SS all round us, machine guns trained: the traditional ceremony. Three victims in chains—and one of them, the little servant, the sad-eyed angel.
>
> The SS seemed more preoccupied, more disturbed than usual. To hang a young boy in front of thousands of spectators was no light matter. The head of the camp read the verdict. All eyes were on the child. He was lividly pale, almost calm, biting his lips. The gallows threw its shadow over him.
>
> This time the *Lagerkapo*[190] refused to act as executioner. Three SS replaced him.
>
> The three victims mounted together onto the chairs.
>
> The three necks were placed at the same moment within the nooses.
>
> "Long live liberty!" cried the two adults.
>
> But the child was silent.
>
> "Where is God? Where is He?" someone behind me asked.
>
> At a sign from the head of the camp, the three chairs tipped over.
>
> Total silence throughout the camp. On the horizon the sun was setting.
>
> "Bare your heads!" yelled the head of the camp. His voice was raucous. We were weeping. "Cover your heads!"

Then the march past began. The two adults were no longer alive. Their tongues hung swollen, blue-tinged. But the third rope was still moving; being so light, the child was still alive. . . .

For more than half an hour he stayed there, struggling between life and death, dying in slow agony under our eyes. And we had to look him full in the face. He was still alive when I passed in front of him. His tongue was still red, his eyes not yet glazed.

Behind me, I heard the same man asking: "Where is God now?"

And I heard a voice within me answer him: "Where is He? Here He is—He is hanging here on this gallows. . . ."

That night the soup tasted of corpses.[191]

Nobel Prize Author Francois Mauriac describes a moving encounter with the young Weisel for whom the terrible event of the Holocaust raised an equally terrible question of God. He writes:

And I, who believe that God is love, what answer could I give my young questioner, whose dark eyes still held the reflection of that angelic sadness which had appeared one day upon the face of the hanged child? What did I say to him? Did I speak of that other Israeli, his brother, who may have resembled him—the Crucified, whose Cross has conquered the world? Did I affirm that the stumbling block to his faith was the cornerstone of mine, and that the conformity between the Cross and the suffering of men was in my eyes the key to that impenetrable mystery whereon the faith of his childhood had perished? . . . We do not know the worth of one single drop of blood, one single tear. All is grace. If the Eternal is the Eternal, the last word for each one of us belongs to Him. This is what I should have told this Jewish child. But I could only embrace him, weeping.[192]

Out of circumstances such as these we needed either to cease doing theology altogether or to do theology differently. We needed a new starting point in response to the obvious presence and senselessness of evil in the world. How are we to think about these things? Where are we to start?

A starting point. Theological dialogue about the suffering of God originated not surprisingly in a Germany that was enslaved by the Nazi regime and in a Japan devastated by the destruction and defeat of World War II. The memories of the latter, I think, are of atomic bombs dropped on Hiroshima and Nagasaki, but Tokyo lost more people in a firebombing than the number of those who perished in either of the two atomic bombs. In Germany, about 130,000 people died in a single night in Dresden.[193]

Several decades later I heard a personal story reflecting upon this event when I was at a conference at Miessen in what was then East Germany. The English translation for the title of the program was "The Decisive Year 1945: Collapse or Liberation." The people convening the event had invited people of every decade of life up to their 80s, and they put us into groups reflecting the various decades. They then asked people who were sixty and seventy and eighty years old, who could remember forty years back to the Hitler years, to tell their own stories of May 1945 and the end of the war.

Wolfgang Ullman, who was a professor of church history at the theological seminary in Berlin and who had spent a quarter with us at Trinity Lutheran Seminary, delivered one of the lectures at the conference. He talked about the text that says that if you silence the children, the stones will cry out, and linked it to his experience during the war. He grew up about ten kilometers from Dresden—that's six miles. He was living there with his mother when the firebombing occurred in February of 1945. Dresden had no military significance at all. It was jammed with refugees who were fleeing from Russian armies that were closing in from the east. Nothing else of any significance was going on there. Two days after the bombing, Ullman and his mother headed for Dresden because his grandparents were living there, and the two needed to see if their family had survived. They were walking because there was no transportation. As they approached the city, he saw what he first thought were piles of stones. The closer they approached, the clearer the objects became—until he discovered to his horror that they were skulls. In the firebombing they had been swept together: That's what happens in a firestorm. The piles of skulls and bones had just been swept together. They stopped by walls or portions of walls, here or there. So Ullman talked about what these stones, these human skulls might say, as one asks the question of the conference—whether what was going on was liberation or collapse. Incidents such as the one he experienced led him to conclude that it was neither; it was just unvarnished evil that we are able to inflict upon one another.

Out of that period in Germany and similar experiences in Japan theological language concerning the suffering of God came into print. One of the books that we need to pay attention to is Bonhoeffer's 1943-44 *Letters and Papers from Prison*. I've always wondered why they didn't use the German title, *Wiederstand und Ergebung,* which in English means *Resistance and Resignation*. That would be a better book title. They were referring to the period before Bonhoeffer went into prison when he was in the Resistance. In prison, he learned to resign himself, to surrender himself, to a will of God over which he could no longer administer or effectuate; he had no freedom to do that. So Bonhoeffer wrote:

> God lets himself be pushed out of the world on to the cross.
> He is weak and powerless in the world, and that is precisely
> the way, the only way, in which he is with us and helps us.
> Matt. 8:17 makes it quite clear that Christ helps us, not by
> virtue of his omnipotence, but by virtue of his weakness and
> suffering. . . . Only the suffering God can help. . . . That is
> a reversal of what the religious man expects from God. Man
> is summoned to share in God's sufferings at the hands of a
> godless world.[194]

Here we see Bonhoeffer's thoughts concerning the evil that was the foundation of World War II. One year later, Japanese Lutheran theologian Kazoh Kitamori published his influential book, *Theology of the Pain of God*. He writes:

> The heart of the gospel was revealed to me as the "pain of
> God." This revelation led me to the path which the prophet

Jeremiah had trod. . . . I am filled with gratitude because I was allowed to experience the depths of God's heart with Jeremiah. . . . What is salvation? Salvation is the message that our God enfolds our broken reality. . . . Luther sees "God fighting with God" at Golgotha (*da streydet Gott mit Gott*). "God opened the way for man's atonement by experiencing unspeakable suffering, going through agonies, and offering himself as sacrifice." The doctrine of atonement is to illumine this process of his agonies. . . . The task of the "theology of the pain of God" is to win over the theology which advocates a God who has no pain.[195]

At the end of this passage he is referring to overcoming scholastic interpretations of God with a more relevant "theology of the pain of God." The powerful nature of this approach for him is revealed when Kitamori writes, "What is salvation? Salvation is the message that our God enfolds our broken reality." This points to the question for us today: How and with what meaning can Christian theology speak of the suffering of God?

Divine Life. The answer is that the suffering of God is grounded, understood and meaningful through claims we can make about the Trinity. Eberhard Jüngel is a good place to start:

> The doctrine of the Trinity is the indispensable, and indispensably difficult, expression of the simple truth that God lives. The expression of this simple truth is indispensably difficult because the certainty that "God lives" must prove itself in the reality of the man Jesus of Nazareth who is proclaimed, believed, and confessed as God. And that certainly means that the certainty that "God lives" must prove itself in the *death* of this man who belongs to God. That is not only because the life of this man includes the fatal end of a human life; rather, because in the fatal end of this human life the beginning of a new relationship to God for all people is grounded! The death of Jesus opens a new relationship to God because it discloses

the *being of God* in its *divine* vitality, on the basis of the death of Jesus. The deity of the living God—the divinity of his life and thus the vitality of God—is compatible in a very precise sense with the death of this human life.

God's life is compatible with the death of Jesus in that it *bears* it. And by taking death on himself, he conquers it. As the victor over death, God discloses himself as God. In that the living God in his deity bears the death of Jesus, in that he burdens the eternity of his being with the crucifixion of Jesus, he demonstrates his divine being as a *living* unity of life and death. The faith which is obligated to the living God for the certainty which was proven in the death of Jesus, proclaims and tells the tension which defines the being of God itself, the tension between eternal life and temporal death, as the story of Jesus Christ. And it thinks and confesses this story in the concept of the triune God.[196]

Nobody in all of my college and seminary years would ever have said that the *being of God* and the vitality of the divine disclose itself on the basis of the death of Jesus! Nobody! New insights are going on here. And Jüngel is saying that one needs more than the figure of Jesus to account for the cross as something that happens to God—and in this chapter I want to say *how* that is so.

At this point, I want to say that if God incorporates the death of Jesus into the being of God, then our language about God must be larger than simply language about Jesus. Language about Jesus in itself is not adequate—but it is the basis. So, the first topic is the freedom of God.

The Freedom of God

The Gospels (that is, the first four books of the New Testament) are to be understood in the context of God's promise arising out of Jesus' crucifixion and resurrection. The promise is that because Jesus has overcome death, all shall live. We come to the texts, then, from the perspective of the final future in which the Son of Man is the Lord of the outcome of history, the judge of the living and the dead.

The cross (that is, the events of crucifixion and resurrection, and the meaning of those events in human history) is the grounding for the Christian confession of God as Trinity. Now, one can confess Jesus as the final judge of history without a necessary confession of God as Trinity. However, when we say that the cross has happened to God, that it represents the death of God, we are required to extend our attention of the cross beyond Jesus' part in it.

The cross and the freedom of God. The event of the cross took place in Jerusalem—and it makes sense in the context of a Jewish understanding of God. Not all peoples shared these interpretations, however. As mentioned earlier, the Greeks, for example, thought divine freedom required a god who is untouched by time and space—that is, a being who has nothing to do with the world and who therefore would be supernatural (that is, transcending nature) and autonomous. This means they expected god and the world to have nothing to do with one another. Some of these notions have been carried down into our own time, and can muddy our ability to understand the Jewish matrix out of which the event of the cross makes sense.

Karl Rahner helps us reconnect with the roots of our faith when he says, "God truly comes to be God in creating that which is united with God and yet also diverse from God." Rahner's point requires God's self-enactment in order for God to be *our* God. That is, God creates and enters history not to know God's Self as God, but to know God's Self as God *pro nobis* (God-for-us). When we talk about the freedom of God in the Christian sense, in the biblical sense, we are talking about the freedom of God to limit God's Self, the freedom to engage in an act of self-limitation—which is exactly what creation means.

A trinitarian theology rooted in salvation history (that is, the history of God's involvement with the creation, including the event of the cross) leads us to think of divine freedom as the freedom of relationship: the freedom of love, not freedom conceived as autonomy and self-sufficiency. Freedom in relationship always entails determination and limitation, freely undertaken as one person binds himself or herself to another in love. In her work on the Triune God, Catherine Mowry LaCugna writes:

In the history of redemption God's freedom mysteriously is the freedom of love and it includes humanity and all of creation as beloved partner. The claim that all this is incidental to God, or that it need not have been so, is not mistaken because it offends human conceit but because it domesticates the mystery of God by restricting divine freedom to an *a priori* idea of what it means to be free. The freedom of the God of Jesus Christ is the freedom of the triune God. The mysteries of God's Covenant with Israel, of the cross and resurrection of Jesus, of new life in the Spirit, form the only solid basis for pondering the nature of God. That is, theology is the contemplation of the divine *oikonomia*.[197]

It is important to make the point here that we take these things so for granted, without asking ourselves, "What do we *mean* when we say God is free?" Or, "What do we *mean* when we say God is creator?" In short, that which we are learning again and again is that we must ask ourselves *not* how to bring words which we already have defined to bear on God, but how do we bring the revelation that has occurred in Christ to bear on the words and meanings that we use for God. That is what we are trying to do: *not* apply God to Jesus, but rather, apply what we know to be true about Jesus to God. This position is the basis for asking, then, how we are to understand the freedom of God—freedom perceived from the basis of our understanding that Jesus is God. And the answer is that *this* freedom, God's freedom, is freedom *for* the world.

Freedom of Creator God. If God is creator and the world is creation, how are we called to be for the world? Here we again are making a differentiation between a Greek understanding of what is meant by god and a Jewish understanding of God.

The Greeks thought of the world as emanation, as something that emanates from God. Well, then we need to ask, "What is an emanation?" The sun emits light, but the sun does not *will* the light that emanates from its nuclear reactions. The Greeks thought of the world as an emanation from God's pure beingness: unintended, unwilled, unwanted, and, in the last analysis, unloved. Out of this comes their notion that death was escape from this world, flight out of the world, a kind of blessed release from the world.

By contrast, the Jewish concept of the creation is not "emanation," as if it were something that could happen without volition. The fact that the world is "creation" means that it is intended by God, wanted by God, willed into existence by God.

Creation also reflects back upon the creator. When we think of creating, we think about calling something into existence, the way an artist creates out of his or her imagination. When I was in Austria in August of 1956, I brought back a lovely statue of a Madonna and child. We were students in Salzburg, and we didn't have any money. But the year was the 200th anniversary of the birth of Mozart, and the Salzburg Festival celebrating the event was in full swing. That day, we walked up to the castle high above the town and there came across a woodcarver's studio. I saw some of the loveliest pieces of carved wooden art I had ever seen, and I wanted to buy one, but I had only the equivalent of twenty bucks, which was far less than the stated price. The next morning, I climbed back up again to that studio and talked to the man who was sweeping up the chips from his floor—and it turned out to be the artist! We had a wonderful conversation; he was a returning veteran; he had been in the German army on the Russian front; he'd been captured in 1945, spent five years in a Russian POW camp, and came back. His vocation was to restore carved wooden altars in the great Gothic churches as well as other carvings. His rule was to let the piece of wood suggest what would be carved. He did not want to do violence anymore.

I told him that I was interested in purchasing the Madonna, because the Madonna had a carved cloak, completely enveloping both the Madonna and the child. He asked about me, and I told him I was a student, intending to be a Lutheran pastor—but I had only my U.S. $20. Could I buy the Madonna for U.S. $20? He said, yes, if I would promise to tell his story whenever anybody saw the Madonna, because, he said, something of himself goes with everything he creates—which is absolutely true. So I tell the story of this man, Aloysius Wintner, whenever I show that Madonna. We see him in his works of art. That's what it means to create. You can fabricate stuff you don't care about—but you cannot create something that is not part of you.

Hence the freedom of God is not the freedom of autonomy, the freedom of non-involvement, the freedom *from* something. The freedom of God is the freedom of love, the freedom of relationship, the freedom *for* something. It is the freedom to be *for* the other, to be available to and involved with the other.

Freedom and vulnerability. To be free for the other is to be vulnerable. When the artist sold his Madonna woodcarving to me, he took a risk. Would I remember his story and tell people about it? He acted without a guarantee.

We see this in parables, too. Here we can recall the parable of the dishonest steward discussed in Chapter 3. This is a parable of God at the mercy of humanity. The dishonest steward gives up his commission. He knocks off 20 percent or 50 percent, so the renters owe nothing to him. He is then at their mercy and utterly vulnerable.

Such vulnerability is inescapable with authentic love. Authentic love as authentic freedom means that one is vulnerable—for there is no love without vulnerability. If God is free *for* the world, then God can be hurt when the world hurts. Parents understand how this is so. You cannot love your children without being vulnerable, without hurting for them. Torturers have now learned that people can withstand incredible pain themselves— but they will break if pain were to be inflicted upon someone they love. Love makes us vulnerable in that way—to hurt when a loved one hurts.

God can be hurt by the world. And God can hurt for the world, on the world's behalf. In fact, that is what *Godness* means. In Hosea 11:8-9, which we discussed at the beginning of Chapter 2, God says, "How can I give you up, Ephraim?" And then God says, "I can't do it! I cannot because I am God, not a human being." In other words, it is because God is God that God is free to suffer for, on behalf of, the world.

The claim we are making here is that the cross—the events of crucifixion and resurrection—is the grounding for the realization that freedom and vulnerability are not only *possibilities* for God. You see, we could argue the point theoretically. However, we are doing more than claiming the validity of a theory. We are saying that the event of the cross allows us to claim that freedom and vulnerability have occurred, have taken place in history and in the being of God. *They happened!*

The Suffering of God

Arguments about whether or not God suffers can be traced back at least to the third century when early Christian theologians were trying to define what is meant by a Triune God. Sabellius taught patripassionism—the idea that the Father suffered *as the Son*, in the form of the Son, on the cross. He made no distinction between the Father and the Son, but described them as merely different modes or appearances of a single being. The theory was condemned as heretical by orthodox trinitarianism.

In the sixth century, a group referred to as theopaschites were condemned because they held that Jesus had only one nature—a divine nature. They denied Jesus' humanity and said only God suffered on the cross, not a human being.

The existence of these heresies disclose the problematic character of Christian confession within the context of Hellenistic philosophy. Recalling the work of Jaroslav Pelikan, David Lotz writes:

> (Pelikan) argues—convincingly, I think—that early Christian theology achieved a definite victory over classical thought, while stressing that this "triumph of theology" was incomplete. Two doctrines in particular—the immortality of the soul (as distinct from the resurrection of the body) and the absoluteness (ontological immutability/impassibility) of God—are "perhaps the most reliable indications of the continuing hold of Greek philosophy on Christian theology."[198]

The various elaborate christological constructions regarding how we speak of the attributes between the divine and human natures are ways to affirm the full humanity of Jesus (including his suffering and death) and at the same time to affirm the impassibility of God.

The acknowledgment of Jesus as God affirms that Jesus' divinity is *about* his humanity. It is the *human Jesus* who is ultimate, final, and therefore can be confessed as God, as divine. Hence Jesus' death on the cross is something that happens to God.

This claim is consistent with the Jewish confession of God as one who suffers.[199] The question for Christian theology is not *whether* but *how* God suffers in the cross. The answer is that God suffers as the Son, and the Father, and the Holy Spirit.

The cross as the suffering of the Son, the Father and the Holy Spirit. The Gospels describe the Son suffering and dying on the cross (Mark 10:45, and the predictions of the passion: Mark 8:31-33, Luke 12:50, Mark 14:36). Galatians 2:20 reports that the Son gave himself into death. Philippians 2:8 says that Jesus was "obedient" to death, a slave's death on a cross.

The suffering of the Father represents a conflict with Judaism. Martin Marty quotes Yeshayahu Leibowitz's "loathing of Christianity" because "it became the supreme expression of the idolatrous world's abuse of Judaism." For Leibowitz the contrast between Christianity and Judaism can be seen in the clash of their basic symbols: Abraham's binding of Isaac and the crucifixion of Jesus.[200] However, the binding of Isaac is called the *akedah* and, according to Nils Alstrup Dahl, it is the binding, the *akedah,* that is rewarded with the reconciliation, the atonement, between God and Abraham.[201]

In the *akedah*, Abraham expressed a theocentric attitude central to Judaism: Man is willing to sacrifice his son for God.

In contrast, the most prevalent Christian theories of the atonement (especially the "Latin" or "objective" one) are anthropocentric: God sacrifices God's son for humankind.

But is this clash of symbols necessary? In understanding the crucifixion, the key passage for us as Christians is Romans 8:31-32, which says: "What then are we to say about these things? If God is for us, who is against us? He who did not withhold his own Son, but gave him up for all of us, will he not also give us everything else?" The text is obviously a reflection on Genesis 22. But the point is that it is because the Father loves the Son that he is able *in this way*—the way described in John 3:16[202]—to give the Son. The opposite of death is not life but birth—for in birth, we are already given over to death. Our parents give us life, only to give us death. If you are a parent, you have given life to your children and, at the same time, given them death. There is no way out.

The freedom of God to participate in birth and life is also the freedom of God to participate in death. The Father hands the Son over to death, as do all parents when they give their children birth and life, and the Father suffers when that death occurs, when the relationship ends, at least for three days. It is essential here to state that this death was as final and real for the Father as it was for the Son—or what we are speaking of is a chimerical sham.

The freedom of the Son is expressed in the willingness of Jesus to affirm his life and, therefore, the willingness to receive death. The horrific *character* of that death, examined in Chapter 4, as well as the betrayal and abandonment that surrounded it, were all part of the Son's suffering in death.

Finally, the suffering of the Holy Spirit can be understood three ways. First, "Spirit" means "life."[203] If the crucifixion is the death of the Son and the giving over to death by the Father, then the crucifixion is the negation of "Spirit." Secondly, "Spirit" refers to downpayment on the eschaton—the victory of the kingdom of God.[204] But the crucifixion is the triumph of the powers of the old age, the powers of death and sin. Hence the crucifixion is the negation of the victory of the reign of God. Finally, "Spirit" means love, and the "Spirit" is understood as the bond of love between the Father and the Son. In his cry from the cross, Jesus expressed being abandoned by the Father. Hence Jesus experienced alienation between the Father and the Son, the negation of the bond of Love which is Holy Spirit. In all of these ways the Spirit participates in the suffering of God which is the meaning of the crucifixion.

The Suffering of God and Human Sin

In the crucifixion and resurrection of Jesus, God takes on human sin—and overcomes it. How? *"How"* is a question that seeks a step-by-step explanation. Hebrews 2:14-18 points out that Jesus enters into death: Jesus dies. And the resurrection shows that this death is not the end of the story, but that Jesus overcomes death, thereby also overcoming fear of death. Thusly, others may now know this truth.

Sin. In 2 Corinthians, Paul says that God (the Father) made Christ to be "sin for us who did not know sin" (5:21). That is, Jesus and the Father experience the alienation of sin, the power of death, the victory of "law."

Here we recognize that sin is not about morality; it is about alienation. On the cross alienation is taken into God, and God also takes in death. In this event we see the depth of God's mercy. As Forde says, Jesus was crucified because God insists on being merciful. This is why it is important to confess that Jesus was crucified as a messianic claimant—and the kind of Messiah he claimed to be involved gathering the lost, the sinners, and *forgiving* them. In forgiveness, the forgiver *bears* the hurt of the sin: That's what it *means* to forgive!

The cross overcomes sin. The Gospel of the suffering of God is the end of the "law" (that is, our way of justifying ourselves, or our basis for hating ourselves), the end of the power of death (that is, our quest for self-protection at the expense of others), the end of sin (that is, our refusal to trust God, to trust the Gospel).

Because God encompasses all death and sin, the cross is the end of the powers of the "old age." As Paul goes on to say in 2 Corinthians:

> From now on, therefore, we regard no one from a human point of view; even though we once knew Christ from a human point of view, we know him no longer in that way. So if anyone is in Christ, there is a new creation: everything old has passed away; see, everything has become new! All this is from God, who reconciled us to himself through Christ, and has given us the ministry of reconciliation; that is, in Christ God was reconciling the world to himself, not counting their trespasses against them, and entrusting the message of reconciliation to us. So we are ambassadors for Christ, since God is making his appeal through us; we entreat you on behalf of Christ, be reconciled to God. For our sake he made him to be sin who knew no sin, so that in him we might become the righteousness of God.[205]

The "old age" has become passé. We cannot now be alienated from God and God's love. The new age has come, and it is the age of the Holy Spirit.

2 Corinthians 13:14 ("The grace of the Lord Jesus Christ, the love of God, and the communion of the Holy Spirit be with all of you") . . . points to the three absolutely basic qualities in the nature of the Triune God. Grace is the most characteristic quality of Jesus. And the essence of God in his unity is love. . . . But then it does not say "the power of the Holy Spirit," or "the light of the Holy Spirit", or "the purity of the Holy Spirit;" it says "the communion" [Greek: *koinonia*], the in-between-ness, of the Holy Spirit. It is often translated fellowship, but fellowship is the result which we can see and feel. What *causes* the fellowship is the gift of awareness which opens our eyes to one another, makes us see as we never saw before, the secret of all evolution, the spark that sets off most revolution, the dangerous life-giver, the Holy Spirit.

John V. Taylor, *The Go-Between God*[206]

CHAPTER 7

THE HOLY SPIRIT

The Holy Spirit is the promise of Jesus given to the eschatological community that we call "church." Wherever in this community we observe or experience the witness of the people to Jesus as Messiah—either in relationship to one another, or in relationship to the society, or in relationship to the whole created world—in the midst of all of these circumstances and events is the presence of the Holy Spirit.

The use of the term "spirit" in religion confronts Christian theology with a number of problems. One problem arises out of the fact that we live within a worldview which no longer understands the term "spirit" as it was intended in the first century. When worldview changes (as it did with the Enlightenment), language no longer refers to the objects or ideas originally attached to it—or, worst of all, it loses its currency altogether. That is, words no longer represent or thematize or explain a relationship to the way we experience our world.

Another problem is compartmentalization: Today, the language of the "spirit" belongs to religion, but is not necessarily understood occurring in daily life. Rather, the word "spirit" is often simply tolerated as part of Christian jargon or ideology.

And a third problem is the attempt to use "spirit" language as an explanation of a coincidence or of the apparently miraculous—which would have been consistent with the way people saw the world 300 years ago, but certainly doesn't make sense today. For example, a big sign posted in front of the little shopping center near my house says, "Holy Spirit rallies tonight. Come and experience miracles!" The offering is an incredible example of an attempt to live in a *pre*-modern world. But it is inconsistent with our expectations of the meaning of "spirit" in the twenty-first century!

The task. Theological attention to the doctrine of the Holy Spirit must be addressed in three parts. The first part is to restore experiential content to the term "spirit" so that it has meaning in a modern context. A second aspect of the task is to relate the Holy Spirit to the eschatological event which has taken place in Jesus, the risen Messiah. Finally, the third task is to understand the relationship of the Holy Spirit to the Father and to the Son in the Holy Trinity; this aspect of the task must include attention to the meaning of the creedal confession of the Holy Spirit as "Lord and giver of life."

Language and Conceptual Problems with the Term "Spirit"

We begin our discussion of the meaning of Holy Spirit by considering how the terms "spirit," "Holy Spirit," "spirituality," and "evil spirit" are understood from the perspective of the modern secular world. The modern secular world prevails if our daily lives understand the supernatural realm as fundamentally irrelevant or even non-existent; from this view, the traditional use of the term "spirit" (whether divine or demonic) does not contain experiential meaning. We do not readily know what experiences are expressed by the religious use of the term "spirit," especially when the term is connected with adjectives like "Holy Spirit" or "evil spirit."

Confusion arising out of this circumstance is compounded by the legacy of Platonic philosophy. Platonic philosophy contrasted "spirit" and "matter" so as to preserve the "perfection" of what Plato perceived to be the real (i.e. ideal) world. One always has to remember that for Plato the real world was thought to be the world outside the material world—so then the material world in which we live was said to be a shadow of reality. This would mean that the chairs you sit on are not as real as the *idea* of a chair. The idea is the reality, not its manifestation, said Plato, and, he posited, we mirror that reality, albeit imperfectly. As a result, a sharp dichotomy exists between the real world (the ideal world, the world that exists in the mind, in the spirit) and the solid, material world.

The reason why this was important to Plato was to preserve reality from the ravages of time. From his perspective, "matter"—which is subject to decay and death—involves change and, therefore, imperfection. Moltmann explained what was going on with Plato's argument when he said, "The Greek word *pneuma*, the Latin *spiritus*, and the Germanic *Geist*/ghost were always conceived as antitheses to matter and body. They mean something immaterial. Whether we are talking Greek, Latin, German, or English, by the Spirit of God we then mean something disembodied, supersensory, and supernatural."[207]

Plato's theory is nearly opposite of our conception or worldview today. We say that our experiential, material world is the real world: This chair that I'm sitting on, this wood that I can knock, this flesh that I can feel—these are real. This means that from the perspective of our materialistic world, a spiritual realm devoid of matter is either unintelligible or irrelevant or both. We understand reality as tangible, quantifiable, and that which can be grasped and measured in the here and now.

Our challenge lies as much with the inaccuracies of the Platonic perspective as with our limiting focus on reality as only that which is tangible. We seem incapable of dealing with both the Jewish understanding of the *ruach* of God ("God is a tempest, a storm, a force in body and soul, humanity and nature," writes Moltmann[208]) and the eschatological Spirit, a presence in history. Our task in theology is to clarify the meaning of the biblical use of the word "spirit" so that it is both intelligible and relevant.

Platonism and piety. Platonism had a profound and continuing influence on Western piety. Our access to Plato's thinking comes to us through Augustine. When we rely on Augustine, we recognize the development of Christianity within a culture other than its origin. We are looking at the development of Christianity, which comes out of Judaism, but which was being adopted through Greek and Roman cultures some 300 years after Christ. Moltmann recognizes the impact of this shift:

> In the degree to which Christianity cut itself off from its Hebrew roots and acquired Hellenistic and Roman form, *it lost its eschatological hope and surrendered its apocalyptic alternative to "this world" of violence and death.* It merged into

late antiquity's gnostic religion of redemption. From Justin onwards, most of the Fathers revered Plato as a "Christian before Christ" and extolled his feeling for the divine transcendence and for the values of the spiritual world. God's eternity now took the place of God's future, heaven replaced the coming kingdom, the spirit that redeems the soul from the body supplanted the Spirit as "the well of life," the immortality of the soul displaced the resurrection of the body, and the yearning for another world became a substitute for changing this one.[209]

Moltmann is pointing to the impact of translating the meaning of Christianity, the meaning of God's promise given through the event of the cross, to a people who had no background in Judaism and, therefore, saw the world through quite different lenses.

If we fast-forward to today, we see the implications of the strain in trying to translate Jewish concepts for a non-Jewish world. Harold Bloom calls quintessential American religion a contemporary form of Gnosticism.[210] He refers here to salvation religions which represent conservative revivalist theology, such as Southern Baptists, Mormons, and Seventh Day Adventists. Among the characteristics of these faiths is the idea of redeeming one *out of* this material world.

We, too, have some strains of this in the Lutheran faith. I grew up with a hymn that included the phrase, "I am but a stranger here, Heaven is my home, Earth is a desert drear, Heaven is my home."[211] It was a dreadful hymn, characteristic of this Gnostic piety—and thankfully was not included in the *Lutheran Book of Worship*.

Out of this background we see two elements which affected Western piety. First, "spirituality" came to mean a quest for God: You, the individual, go looking for God; and then you seek disengagement from "the world." The people who were considered the most pious were those who were the least worldly—so that the highest degree of piety was the greatest ability to disengage yourself from the material world. If you really wanted to be a pious Christian, you went into a monastery: You lived the holiest kind of life, you didn't marry, and you didn't own property. You see, the more spiritual a person became, the less that person would be involved in the world, its institutions, its problems and needs, its hopes and expectations—that was piety! All of this is, of course, a misinterpretation of the meaning of "spirit" or "spirituality" arising out of centuries of false interpretations. For us, the point we need to remember is that when we use the word "spirituality" today we must be very careful how we define what we are doing.

Misinterpretations contributing to the problem. The worldview in the Bible assumes a spirit realm (a realm that includes God, the angelic, the demonic) acting upon and controlling the material, human, earthly realm.[212] For example, Matthew 8:28-34 describes Jesus' expulsion of spirits from the demoniacs: The spirits asked to be sent into the pigs; Jesus gives them permission; and they inhabit the pigs, who then rush over the edge of the cliff and are destroyed as they tumble into the lake near Gadara. Today this is a crazy story! We do not share that first-century worldview, so we can make no sense of it.

In our day, the intelligibility of the concept of a spirit realm involved in controlling the material world has eroded because we now know so much about *how* the world works; learned disciplines such as medicine, psychology, biology, sociology, and other anthropological natural and social sciences explain many mysteries. For example, if I were to have a convulsion and were thrown to the floor in front of you, you would not, first of all, assume demon-possession; you would assume something else—possibly epilepsy or some medically explicable thing. Or if six of us were in an emergency room with an unexplained malady, we would first try to explain what was happening and run every test. The thought would not cross our minds that we were experiencing a demonic event—even as an absolute last resort, even after having tried everything else, after having cleared everybody out, after having put on heavily insulated suits, after having come in with Geiger counters, after having performed autopsies—we would not think to call a priest to see if an exorcism could be performed. Nobody suggests that! We don't think in terms of the spirit behaving in this way at all!

The result of our confusion over the meaning of "spirit" has been uneasy application of the term—when it is used at all—in our daily lives. We say the words, "In the name of the Father, Son, and Holy Spirit. . . ." Or we might make a militant (defensive) re-assertion of the spirit realm as the antithesis of the human realm. But what does this mean? How do you know—today—that you have been given the gift of the Holy Spirit?

This gift has often been tied to the inexplicable. Episcopal priest Dennis Bennett talks about the gift of the Holy Spirit in terms of his ability to speak languages in which he has had no instruction.[213] None. Not even any prior contact. He cites Japanese as an example. What is interesting is his claim to speak perfect Japanese—grammatically perfect and perfect in vocabulary—as a way of emphasizing the fact that his ability is truly miraculous. He says he is not stumbling and bumbling along, just tossing out a few words: *sayanara,* or whatever could be picked up from watching *Shogun* on television.

Other groups say that it is the "gift of the Holy Spirit" in being able to speak in a "prayer language" unintelligible to almost everyone else. Without deciding the factual basis of the claims made, *to equate* these abilities with the "gift of the Holy Spirit" is a misappropriation of the Spirit's actions. Yet, it is a position held by millions of Christians.

Another example of our uncritical use of the term "spirit" might be a healing for which there is no medical explanation. Or perhaps someone could claim to receive information: He is told something, or says he is led in a certain direction. When people say they can do things for which there is no ordinary, inner-worldly, medical, psychological, or any other explanation, they might as a last resort point to the ability as a sign of the spirit.

Both alternatives—the avoidance of the tradition on the one hand and the uncritical assertion of it in the midst of a modern worldview on the other hand—are theologically and intellectually unsatisfactory. To overcome this challenge, we need to move toward recovery of experiential meaning for the term "spirit."

Recovery of Experiential Meaning for the Term "Spirit"

The initial step toward recovering an experiential meaning for "spirit" is to ask whether the term is still used meaningfully to describe certain experiences from the perspective of our current worldview. Does the term "spirit" (as an organizing category of the mind) have something mediated by the senses to work on?

The use of the term "spirit" in modern culture. The term "spirit" is, in fact, used today, and its usage is not "supernatural" as the opposite of "natural" or "material," nor "superhuman" as the opposite of "human." Rather, the term "spirit" is used to describe an experience which expresses itself *through* the agency of another person and/or community but which nevertheless *transcends* that agency. We might think here of team spirit, mob spirit, community spirit, the spirit of Martin Luther King, Jr., or the spirit of Clara Barton (1821-1912). As an illustration, every time the Red Cross, which she founded, moves in to provide disaster relief in Los Angeles or help for persons suffering from floods in Iowa or hospitals for refugees, there, in the midst of those situations, the spirit of its founder is functioning. So in some sense, we know what that use of the term "spirit" means.

Likewise, the spirit of Martin Luther King, Jr. (1929-1968) is recalled every January when we watch the television reports of the 1963 "I have a dream" speech. Fruits of his work, his spirit, also are evident in the Civil Rights legislation of 1964-65.

One also sees the use of the term "team spirit" in the headlines. One morning we read that Indiana suffered its worst basketball defeat in Bobby Knight's history—to Minnesota! (Yahoo! Minnesota beat Indiana by fifty points last night! You've got to be from Minnesota to love it.) And now come the attempted explanations—but you can't predict rebounds and three-point baskets, and all these good things. So you give it up to team spirit. You can see it when it's present, and it points to that which is functioning among the players on the floor, working in a way that transcends stacking up all the individual abilities and qualities of the players.

Another example comes from my own experience. Back in the early 1950s, Fort Leonard Wood in Missouri was the basic training camp for people being sent to the Korean War. Every week for the eight-week program, one-eighth of the people coming into the camp were new. Many were college-aged servicemen, and they included some of the finest basketball players in the country. They would organize a pick-up game just for recreation and schedule games: the Fort Leonard Wood All-Stars with Anybody-Who-Wanted-to-Play-Them. Person for person, our seminary team was never as good as these all-stars, but we beat them every year because we had a team with spirit. We can say that this quality made us a better team than the individual abilities of any of the players on either end of the floor.

On the negative side, we might think of the actions of a mob. Reinhold Niebuhr said that people will do things in a group that they would never do as individuals. We allow ourselves to vent anger, outrage, hostility, or act on murderous impulses as a mob in ways that we would never demonstrate as individuals. We might be caught up by a spirit that we are not able to explain or understand even to ourselves. For example, a British reporter who hated Hitler and Naziism went to Nuremburg, Germany, in 1936 to attend one of the party rallies. He sat among 250,000 people in a stadium surrounded by 160 floodlights. The lights were focused straight up; at night they seemed like white columns holding up the sky so that everyone there experienced the vastness of the space. Into the stadium marched the military units with their torches, a mass of flags, and all of the standards and banners that Hitler revived from the Roman Empire. People joined in singing songs. Speeches warmed up the crowd until finally, when they were at fever pitch, Hitler came bounding up out of a room below the stage, up onto this immense tribune—and the whole huge assembly leaped to its feet, shouting a Hitler salute: Heil! Heil! And the reporter found himself doing it, too, alongside everybody else—and then he said to himself, "What am I doing?" And he backed off, but realized he had been caught up in—now listen to the words—"the spirit of the moment."

That's how people experienced what they were doing.

Here we see the use of the word spirit to express the spirit "of" something. It is something which functions in a community or through a community, but nevertheless transcends the sum total of the people involved. The focus is on the *quality* of the person or community in operation, whether destructive or redemptive, whether "holy" or "unholy." Please note that I am still not using capital letters here. The adjective is dependent upon the quality of the event that is occurring. For example, Gerhard Ebeling wrote, "Further explanation is needed in order that we may not confuse the courage of despair with the courage of faith, the spirit of evil with the Holy Spirit. For the 'courage of faith' means the Holy Spirit."[214]

Robert Jenson points out that the question of the church is to ask the source of the spirit: Which spirit animates an experience?

> As the creed addresses its *doxological* predicates to the Father, and adorns the Son with *titles*, so it provides *specification* of the Spirit. It is always a question about a spirit: which spirit is this? Whose spirit is this? The Apostles' creed—always more economical than others—has just one specifying adjective: this spirit is "holy." That is, he [sic] is God's spirit and therefore *not* one of the numerous spirits of this variously and ambiguously animated creation. "Spiritual experience" may as well be of a devil as of God, depending on its content; to be in *this* Spirit, the Spirit the creed has in mind, is to be disciples of the one whose Spirit he is, of the Lord Jesus and none other.[215]

I would say it this way: The Holy Spirit is the eschatological gift (that is, the experience) of the eschatological Messiah, Jesus of Nazareth, for the eschatological community (the church).

The Promise of the Spirit in the Ministry of Jesus

Our claims about the Spirit must begin with Jesus, for it is our claim that Jesus is God which informs our understanding of God's promises. Thus far, we have said that the resurrection disclosed Jesus to be the eschatological Messiah, who is Lord because death no longer has dominion over him (Romans 6:9), and who can therefore be confessed as God.

The death and resurrection of Jesus reveal that already the messianic age has been inaugurated. The promise of that messianic age, and the church's language and experience of the Holy Spirit, are grounded in Jesus as the eschatological messiah. We recall that the signs of this age become apparent when Jesus did messianic works by the power of the Holy Spirit. Matthew 12:28 is just one example among many in which we are told that Jesus' ministry on behalf of the reign of God involves conflict with and victory over demons and the reign of the Prince of Demons.[216]

This age becomes even more real and pervasive after the resurrection. Jesus promises his irrevocable presence in the eschatological messianic commission to make disciples of the nations through baptism in the Triune Name—a Name which includes the Holy Spirit (Matthew 28:16-20). Through the presence of the Holy Spirit, the baptized community will bring in the reign of God to the whole world.

Teach us to pray. As the disciples gather around Jesus, they ask him to unite them with their own prayer (Luke 11). In the context of the day, a rabbi and a circle of disciples understood that one of the functions of prayer was its role as a badge or a distinguishing characteristic among followers. It could have been a prayer taken from the synagogue liturgies, or it could have been one specifically designed for the occasion. The point is that when the disciples say, "Lord, teach us to pray, as John taught his disciples," they don't mean teach us how to engage in the act of praying. They mean, give us a prayer! Give us our *own* symbolic prayer! And then Jesus gives them, "Father, hallowed be your name, your kingdom come," and so on. Both of these petitions come from the *kadish*, but in the synagogue service, the words are "*may* your kingdom come yet"—which is a *request* for something to come in our lifetime. By contrast, the prayer given by Jesus *recognizes* that the kingdom *is here*. God's name *is being* hallowed. In the ancient Syriac version, the words are also "Give us tomorrow's bread *already today*." That is, put us at the eucharistic messianic banquet table. The prayer is eschatological throughout, and is followed by a parable about the importunate servant who storms heaven with his requests.[217] Then in verses 9 and 10 Jesus says, "So I say to you, ask and it will be given you; search and you will find, knock and the door will be opened, for everyone who asks receives, everyone who searches finds, and for everyone who knocks, the door will be opened." In a way, you can think of this as an eschatological blank check: You want to be in on the reign of God? Come! You don't have to stand in line! No waiting list! *And it is in this context that the Spirit will be given.*

The inauguration of the messianic age. The book of Acts begins with narratives of Jesus that are both reference to and promise of the Holy Spirit. Jesus' instructions to the apostles are "through the Holy Spirit" (Acts 1:2). Likewise, the text says that "John baptized with water, but you will be baptized with [or by] the Holy Spirit not many days from now" (Acts 1:5). And, "you will receive power when the Holy Spirit has come upon you" (Acts 1:8).

The Holy Spirit also is referenced through symbolic language expressive of the Jewish *ruach*. In Acts 2 and 3, the presence of the Holy Spirit is compared to a sound "like the rush of a violent wind" (Acts 2:2). Elsewhere, tongues "as of fire" indicate that this is the eschatological Spirit, the Spirit of judgment and the purification of Israel. The entire group gathered here experiences the Spirit, for all are speaking "as the Spirit gave them ability" (Acts 2:4). The text reflects back to Joel 2:28-29, in which the promise is recorded for all Israel, indeed for "all flesh." The event is catholic—that is, it is universal—for the languages are spoken "so that we hear, each of us, in our own native language." Moreover, the text is a communal reversal of the alienating event of the Tower of Babel (Genesis 11:1-9). Remember that in Genesis the people are scattered by languages. Here, they are brought together by a great linguistic event.

The Spirit in this context also points to the end of patriarchal oppression. In a patriarchal culture, not only were the women subject to the patriarch, but so were the children—no matter how long they lived or how old they became—until the patriarch died. This rule comes to an end in the age of the Spirit. Indeed, the experience of the Spirit is even for "slaves, both men and women." Likewise, "young men shall see visions," as well as "old men shall dream dreams." Daughters as well as sons "shall prophesy." Note here that the *whole community* is called to be "prophetic"—that is, they are called not to predict the future but to *announce* God's future! *They* are *inspired* to *announce* the reign of God!

The Advocate. The Gospel of John reports Jesus' promise of an "Advocate" to hold you up when your legs are weak or crumbling. The promise describes this Advocate[218] as one who is "to be with you forever," the "Spirit of Truth" (John 14:16) in contrast to the devil, who is "murderer" and "father of lies" (John 8:44).

The presence and experience of the Spirit is dependent on witness to Jesus as the grounding of redemption—for the Spirit will bear witness to me, Jesus says.[219] The function of leading the disciples into all truth ("inspiration") refers to insight into what they have experienced (John 16:13-15). This does not mean that they will receive thoughts they did not think before; rather, *they will understand events in a new way.* They will see what the crucifixion and resurrection were all about. They will experience that "Aha!" moment—an "Aha!" about the redemptive nature of Jesus as crucified Messiah—*that's* Holy Spirit, *that's* inspiration (John 14:1-7; 14:25-28; and 16:1-15).

Also in this Gospel we find that the promise of the Spirit is associated with the forgiveness of sins. Forgiveness means new possibilities in the midst of the old bondage; it means second chances. Jesus breathes on them—again, a reference to *ruach*—and says, "Receive the Holy Spirit." And then he says, the sins you forgive are forgiven, and the sins you don't aren't. In other words, the reign of God is not going to happen if *you* do not do it (John 20:19-23).

Pentecost Event: Spirit and Community

The question we want to address now that we have language for "spirit" is how we ought to describe experience of the Spirit so that it makes sense in the twenty-first century. That is, how does the presence of the Holy Spirit inform our lives today?

Acts and the apostolic letters discuss how the event of the cross grounds claims that the messianic age is inaugurated, and then go on to describe how an understanding of the messianic age gives people courage to live in new ways—ways which expect and glorify the presence of the Spirit in the midst of the community.

In Romans 8:1-27, for example, Paul asserts a decisive eschatological change. He says there is "now no condemnation" for those in Christ Jesus. Contrary to what has always been (such as the old pre-Christ human situation he discusses in Romans 7), we no longer fear that our lives will have been without value. And the reason is that the standard of judgment has changed. Jenson writes, "Once we were judged in a way that convicted of sin and sentenced to death and by which, therefore, sin and death maintained their control; now we are judged in a way that frees for life and by which, therefore, the *Spirit* rules, the opposite of death and bondage."[220]

So here we have a penultimate outcome of God's act in Christ. The penultimate outcome here points to the existence of two kinds of people: those still in the situation before the great change who still live "according to the flesh" and those who live "according to the Spirit." The point is not to contrast materiality with piety. When Paul uses the word "flesh," he means those who live "according to a way which is in opposition to God." The other kind of people, however, share a worldview which understands the meaning of the event of the cross and the inauguration of the messianic age: That is what it means to live according to the Spirit. Again, Jenson is instructive: ". . . life 'according to flesh' is . . . life that holds its breath, that tries to be purpose and energy for itself. Life 'according to Spirit' is life that rejoices in being moved and inspired by God. . . ."[221]

In verses 9 to 11, Paul shifts the language of the text from third person to second person. He gets carried away, and he says to them, "But you are not in the flesh. You are in the Spirit. Since the Spirit of God dwells in you. . . ." So he is announcing what has in fact happened to them as a community.

The freedom of the Spirit. When the community understands itself as the "society destined to be universal,"[222]—that is, as the eschatological community—then the "Holy Spirit" means the "down payment" which enables the disciple community of Jesus to live in anticipation of the eschaton as if it were already theirs (2 Corinthians 1:22, 5:5; cf. Ephesians 1:14). The Greek word I've cited in those passages is ἀρραβῶνα Θαρρουντες, which refers to a confidence, or earnestness. When you make the down payment on a house, you move in. When you make the down payment on a car, you drive it off the lot and zip down the eschatological highway. You act as if you already own them; they are already "yours." "Holy Spirit" thus means the Spirit of the community which manifests itself as the freedom to live in anticipation of the redemptive reign of God.[223]

The Holy Spirit happens and can be recognized when there is the confession of Jesus as Gospel (1 Corinthians 12:3). You cannot say Jesus is *Lord* except by the Holy Spirit, for to confess Jesus as "Lord" does not mean "lordship" as the world understands it—that would be as the freedom to dominate others or even simply to get out from somebody's domination. Rather, the freedom of the Spirit is now experienced as "sociality." Moltmann says, "I am free and feel free when I am respected and accepted by other people, and when I for my part respect and accept other people too. . . . Then the other person is no longer the limitation of my freedom, but its extension."[224]

This also is Luther's powerful insight in his 1520 spiritual classic, "On the Freedom of a Christian," in which he writes, "A Christian is a perfectly free lord of all, subject to none. A Christian is a perfectly dutiful servant of all, subject to all."[225] We call this Luther's double thesis: If you are first subject, then you will always fear: Will people like me enough? Or am I doing my duty enough? Or am I safe from the powers of death in some way? And the result is that you will not then be free. Only if you are fully *free in the Spirit* can you then be subject to others and serve them truly. So, for example, Bonhoeffer was free to plot against Hitler, even though he was eventually executed for it. And in his freedom, he served Germany better than his executioners.

Hence, the "fruits of the Spirit" indicate that the eschatological community is a community of unconditional acceptance and commitment (1 Corinthians 12-14, Galatians 5:16-26, etc.). And what are the fruits of the Spirit? Galatians tells us they are love, joy, peace, gentleness, meekness, patience, self-control, and so on. Against these, there is no law, Paul says, smiling, laughing out loud.

All of this makes the church a "contrast-society,"[226] in which the spirit of this particular community is the Holy Spirit. We then conclude: Where something like eschatological anticipation is happening in the witness of the church to Jesus as Messiah, in the relationship of Christians to each other, and in the relationship of Christians to society and the whole created world—this is the gift of "Holy Spirit."

The intention and consequence of the doctrine of the Trinity is not only the deification of Christ; it is even more the Christianization of the concept of God.

Jürgen Moltmann, *The Trinity and the Kingdom*[227]

CHAPTER 8

THE TRINITY AND LANGUAGE FOR GOD

The word "Trinity" identifies God.

The identification of "God" has been the focus of our attention throughout history. It was the focus of major discussions among early church fathers who sometimes charged one another with heresies. In time, they wrote creeds to formally define how the new church was to think about its shared understanding of God—and still, questions arose.

The concept of a Triune God is one of the most difficult in Christian theology, so we continue to ask today: "What does it mean to say that God is Triune?"

What is at stake in the study of the doctrine of the Trinity can be seen in these two versions of a familiar doxology:

> Praise God, from whom all blessings flow;
> Praise him [sic], all creatures here below;
> Praise him [sic] above, ye heav'nly host;
> Praise Father, Son, and Holy Ghost.
>
> *Thomas Ken (1637-1711)*

> Praise God from whom all blessings flow;
> Praise Christ, all people here below;
> Praise Holy Spirit evermore,
> Praise Triune God, whom we adore.
>
> *Contemporary revision*

Is the orthodoxy of the doctrine of the Trinity being challenged by the second version? Does it reflect an appropriate development of the doctrine of the Trinity? Is the Christian Gospel being confessed in both versions? These are among the questions which must be addressed as we consider the Trinity and language for God.

The task. The doctrine of the Trinity is the way we must speak of God, tell the story of God, if in fact the Christian Gospel is true. Faith in the Gospel determined the development of the doctrine of the Trinity in the ancient church. Likewise today, only attention to the Gospel character of the doctrine of the Trinity can disclose its existential power and its ability to shape faithful Christian discipleship.

The authentic doctrine of the Trinity has its grounding and meaning in Jesus—specifically, in the cross of Jesus—that is, language which by now we know refers to crucifixion and resurrection events of Jesus. The Trinity is confessed in the creeds and the confessions of the church as expressions of faith in the Gospel.[228] And the Trinity is the way we must think of God if the cross of Jesus is something that has happened to God.

This chapter begins with recognition of the problems which arise when we do not have adequate language for God. It then continues with an explanation of what we mean when we claim that the doctrine of the Trinity is grounded in Jesus, the Christ. It will look at a brief review of much of what we have already covered, but focusing on grounding for our claim that God is revealed as a Trinity. It will show how our understanding of Jesus as "Son" opens possibilities for understanding the Triune God, and finally, close with the meaning of the oneness of God.

Twenty-first Century Confusion about Language for God

Interest in the doctrine of the Trinity, at least in the United States, has to do with a number of cultural phenomena which have seriously impacted the Christian churches of this country—among them, pluralism and feminism. Martin Marty's second volume in his history of American religion in the twentieth century, the *Noise of Conflict, 1919-1941*,[229] tells the story of how American Protestantism came to share "the power to influence" with the Roman Catholic Church in the decades between the two world wars. After the Second World War, Judaism made it a triumvirate. By 1976, Marty's *A Nation of Behavers*[230] called for a "new map" of

American religion. Islam, Asian religions, and ethnic religions were publicly evident. The charismatic movement was here to stay. Evangelicalism and fundamentalism were challenging the mainline denominations. In the 1980s, "new age" religions proliferated and caught on.

In the midst of visible pluralism, theologians began asking about the identity of the term "god," a new and startling question for both nominal and active Christians. In response, Robert Bellah said that concepts of God—that is, our identifications of God—have "grown cancerous" with individualism, and are therefore eclectic, arbitrary, and idiosyncratic.

Bellah reported on one woman's idea:

> I believe in God. I'm not a religious fanatic. I can't remember the last time I went to church. My faith has carried me a long way. It's Sheilaism. Just my own little voice. It's just try to love yourself and be gentle with yourself. You know, I guess, take care of each other. I think He [sic] would want us to take care of each other.[231]

Bellah then explained:

> Radically individualistic religion, particularly when it takes the form of a belief in cosmic selfhood, may seem to be in a different world from conservative or fundamentalist religion. Yet these are the two poles that organize much of American religious life. To the first, *God is simply the self magnified*; to the second, *God confronts man* [sic] *from outside the universe.* One seeks a self that is finally identical with the world; the other seeks an external God who will provide order in the world. Both value personal religious experience as the basis of their belief. Shifts from one pole to the other are not as rare as one might think. The two experiences that define the faith of "Sheila Larson" took a similar form. Going into major surgery, God spoke to her to assure her that all would be well, but the voice was her own. Once, nursing a dying woman, Sheila had the experience that "if she looked in the mirror" she "would see Jesus Christ."[232]

But the "Christ" vision she would "see" would be distorted through mere anachronistic projection, with God as the cosmic micro-manager of individual lives and destinies. Not only is there no "grand narrative" in place with this approach to God; there is no objective narrative at all! What matters supremely is subjective experience, our "personal testimony." We can argue over whether the various religions' competing narratives are true or false. However, individualism's relativizing dimension means there is no longer anything with which to argue. We are individually our own religious experts.

Another expression of culture's individualistic attitude toward God is identified by Harold Bloom's "American religion." It is, he asserts, a modern form of "gnosticism":[233]

> Freedom, in the context of the American religion, means being alone with God or with Jesus, the American God or the American Christ. In social reality, this translates as solitude, at least in the inmost sense. The soul stands apart, and something deeper than the soul, the Real Me or self or spark, thus is made free to be utterly alone with a God who is also quite separate and solitary, that is a free God or God of freedom. What makes it possible for the self and God to commune so freely is that the self already is of God.[234]

Note that what is at stake here is a definition of "freedom" as an individual's (or a nation's) "right to self-determination." Such freedom involves the power to protect one's self from others and, if necessary, the right to maintain one's self at the expense of others, in domination and oppression of others: *That* is the link between American "gnostic" religion and a certain vision of America, a certain kind of nationalistic politics. So, you see, it may be that there is not much from which to choose with regard to these cultural options—that is, between the god who is the self and the god with which the self is already in communion.

We also need to recognize that in the context of cultural and religious feminism, the doctrine of the Trinity is a controversial resource. Significant feminist voices challenge not only the evident patriarchalism and sexist suppression of women in the early centuries of Christian history; they also challenge dogmatic definitions of the Trinity and christology as both consequences and tools of patriarchal oppression. The terms "Father" and "Son" for the first and second persons of the Trinity are under attack as making it difficult, if not impossible, for women to identify with the God of orthodox Christian teaching. Furthermore, according to feminist critics, the continued use of such terms for God perpetuates male dominance and oppression in the churches. Sallie McFague, for example, thinks that we can say very little with any confidence about Christianity, that Christianity is basically a claim "that there is a power which is on the side of life," and that "we have some clues for fleshing out this claim in the life, death, and appearances of Jesus of Nazareth." She then proposes the terms "mother, lover, and friend" as more appropriate metaphorical language for God.[235]

So, too, Isabel Carter Heyward rejects classical Christian doctrine and asserts:

> I am not interested in the "God" who batters like a ramrod through the priestly pages of Leviticus and on into the misogynist diatribes of Jerome, Martin Luther, and John Paul II. If this is the "God" of Jews and of Christians, then I must reject Christianity's "God" and the Church that pays "Him" homage.[236]

It is for me a source of great sadness that the history of the treatment of women in Christian churches offers sufficient justification for the feelings behind this rejection of what I believe to be the Christian truth inherent in the dogmas of christology and the Trinity. Living as we do in a culture which seeks to respect all persons, we can no longer assume the tradition (if, indeed, we ever could). We must make choices about the tradition. While the masculine character of language for God is considered controversial by some persons, avoiding masculine language or metaphors altogether does not solve the problem of understanding what is meant by the Trinity. An alternative which is consistent with the good news of the Gospel is language grounded in the resurrected Christ.

The Problem of Scholasticism

In generations past, one did not learn the doctrine of the Trinity as a doctrine of the Gospel. The Lutheran scholastic tradition which I learned both as a boy and as a seminarian taught that there was natural and supernatural knowledge of God. Natural knowledge of God derived from rational observation of the world. Such observation yielded the knowledge that God exists, that God is one, eternal, immutable, infinite, that God was omniscient, immortal, omnipresent, and omnipotent, that God is alone the source of life, holiness, justice, and goodness. The supernatural knowledge of God consisted of the doctrine of the Trinity, that God is one and yet also three—namely, Father, Son, and Spirit. This is supernatural knowledge because it is a mystery which is altogether beyond the grasp of reason.

It is not difficult to see that such an understanding of the doctrine of the Trinity had nothing to do with human experience. It was taught as mathematical/rational nonsense. It became for me a component of Christian ideology, and as such it had to be believed. But in the process it also came to distort the nature of Christian faith. To believe the doctrine of the Trinity became an intellectual exercise, even if the character of that intellectual exercise was the setting aside of normal rational procedures. Making such an act of faith easily came to be regarded as a virtue, especially when one compared oneself with those "unbelievers" who were not ready to sacrifice their rationality.

Such a doctrine of the Trinity could be imposed only in an authoritarian way. My questions about the doctrine of the Trinity were answered with some variation of "Shut up and believe." When the doctrine of the Trinity is taught as an intellectually incomprehensible mystery, then it can only be imposed by means of external authority, either the church or the Bible. Such heteronomy, to employ Tillich's term, substitutes institutional or ideological loyalty for authentic faith. A doctrine so imposed by a patriarchal church cannot avoid being seen as both product and instrument of male hegemony, thus inviting revolt and rejection.

At fault, I believe, is the general construct of the scholastic tradition.[237] The Scriptures of the church cannot function as a textbook of doctrines. And Scriptures do not have a doctrine of the Trinity. Instead, the church was required to give an account of its understanding of God if in fact it believes the witness of the Scriptures to the Gospel. That alone appropriately explains the development of the doctrine of the Trinity.

From Eschatological Event to Trinitarian Dogma

It is now possible to trace the movement toward the dogmatic formulations of the fourth and fifth centuries which emerged from the apostolic eschatological experience and subsequent proclamations of "good news." The first development to be noted is that in the first generation of disciples Jesus is the subject of proclamation and the object of praise and prayer. *Because Jesus has the power of the future,* the salvation of the world can be proclaimed in him. A number of texts could be cited here, among them: "As all die in Adam, so all will be made alive in Christ" (1 Corinthians 15:22), and "God was in Christ reconciling the world to himself" (2 Corinthians 5:19). *Because Jesus has the power of the future,* praise can be addressed to him, as we see in the Christ Hymn which seems to be quoted in Philippians 2:6-11:

> [Christ Jesus], who though he was in the form of God,
> did not regard equality with God
> as something to be exploited,
> but emptied himself,
> taking the form of a slave,
> being born in human likeness,
> And being found in human form,
> He humbled himself
> and became obedient to the point of death—
> even death on a cross.
> therefore God also highly
> exalted him
> and gave him the name
> that is above every name,
> so that at the name of Jesus
> every knee should bend,

in heaven and on earth and
under the earth,
and every tongue should confess
that Jesus Christ is Lord,
to the glory of God the Father.

Likewise, *because Jesus has the power of the future*, prayer can be addressed to him, as in the prayer of the dying proto-martyr Stephen:

While they were stoning Stephen, he prayed, "Lord Jesus, receive my spirit. Then he knelt down and cried out in a loud voice, "Lord, do not hold this sin against them." When he had said this, he died (Acts 7: 59-60).

I have begun three sentences in the previous paragraph with the phrase, "because Jesus has the power of the future" to lead us to the *meaning* of the eventual confession that Jesus is God. In a Jewish context, God is experienced in historical rather than ontological terms. "God" means whoever does something in history which has eschatological power. Thus "God" means whoever blesses Abraham so that in him "all the families of the earth shall be blessed" (Genesis 12:2-3). Translated by Paul, Abraham is the father of all who believe, and "God" means whoever "gives life to the dead and calls into existence the things that do not exist" (Romans 4:16-17). If Jesus has the power of the future, if death does not have the last word in history but rather Jesus has the last word, then *Jesus* now defines what is meant by "God." For "God" means whoever has finality and ultimacy in history.

If "God" means whoever has ultimacy (that is, historical finality), then the confession that Jesus is God is consistent with the confession that Jesus has the power of the future by virtue of his resurrection from the dead. He, and not death, has ultimacy, finality. In the words of an early Christian author, "we ought to think of Jesus Christ as we do of God" (2 Clement 1:1). It is not that we try to apply qualities like "infinity" and "immortality" with which the Hellenistic world defined divinity to the historical Jesus. It is rather that by virtue of his resurrection—which happened: was an event, an action—*Jesus* now defines what we mean by divinity.

Importance of the Jewish matrix. Attention to the good news of the New Testament requires that we focus on the Jewish matrix of Christianity as the path by which Christianity arrived at the doctrine of the Trinity. Affirmation of the Trinity is a response to the historical event of Jesus as the Messiah of Israel. It is how we must tell the story of God if indeed Jesus has been raised from the dead. It is above all how the cross is part of the story of God.

Recall that in Chapter 2 we said that the Jewish matrix requires two things: First, Jesus and his disciples were thoroughly grounded in Jewish scriptures and Jewish life, and above all in Jewish hopes and expectations. Second, we began our understanding of God with the *acts of God* rather than with the *being of God*—that is, we began with what God does and proceeded to implications for what God is; or, said another way, we began with soteriology and proceeded to ontology. The apostolic proclamation of the Gospel from Acts 2 is instructive. Note the trinitarian language in this summary:

> This Jesus God raised up, and of that all of us are witnesses. Being therefore exalted at the right hand of God, and having received from the Father the promise of the Holy Spirit, he has poured out this that you both see and hear. For David did not ascend into the heavens, but he himself says,
>
> > "The Lord said to my Lord,
> > 'Sit at my right hand,
> > until I make your enemies your footstool.'
>
> > "Therefore let the entire house of Israel know with certainty that God has made him both Lord and Messiah, this Jesus whom you crucified" (Acts 2:32-36).

Compare it with Paul's summary of the Gospel as it appears in the opening paragraphs of his letter to the Romans. Note once again the trinitarian language:

> Paul, a servant of Jesus Christ, called to be an apostle, set apart for the Gospel of God, which he promised beforehand

through his prophets in the holy scriptures, the Gospel concerning his Son, who was descended from David according to the flesh and was declared to be Son of God with power according to the Spirit of holiness by resurrection from the dead, Jesus Christ our Lord, through whom we have received grace and apostleship to bring about the obedience of faith among all the Gentiles for the sake of his name, including yourselves who are called to belong to Jesus Christ (Romans 1:1-6).

The summary from Acts refers to Jesus as the one whom God raised up: It is what salvation history tells us God did. The reference of Jesus moves us next to the one identified as his "Father," and to the "Holy Spirit" promised by the Father and "poured out" by Jesus. In Paul's introduction we find a reference to God, to Jesus as the "Son of God," and to the "Spirit of holiness" associated with Jesus' resurrection. Especially noteworthy, however, is the fact that the content of the apostolic "good news" is deceptively simple: Jesus is the Messiah, the Savior. Jesus has been raised from the dead: It is what God did, and therefore, we know God through this act.

Re-envisioning God the Father. The basis for the early confession that Jesus is God is the encounter with the risen Jesus as the eschatological Messiah of Israel, as the "Son of Man," the final judge of history. If our confession is valid, then we must consider the history of Jesus in a new way. That is, we must retrieve the crucifixion of Jesus so that we understand it not only as something that has happened to the Messiah, but also as something that has happened to God.

For the crucifixion to be confessed as something that has happened to God—as belonging essentially to the Christian "good news"—we need more than the christological dogma which began this book: Jesus is God. We need to remember that on the cross Jesus addresses "God" from whom he is alienated. In addition, Jesus' way to the cross and through the cross to the resurrection involves the companionship of the unique and Holy Spirit, the Spirit of authentic freedom and eschatological life of the reign of God.

If Jesus is God and if the crucifixion happens to God, then the Trinity is how we must speak of God if the Gospel is true! This means that whenever in the historical documents of Christian theology the word "God" is used without any other specification, we always think or say: the Triune God or God the Holy Trinity.

We must retrieve Yahweh, the covenant God of Israel's history, as the Eternal Trinity: God the creator and redeemer, who creates and redeems through the Word, and who animates the creation, the nations, and Israel through the unique and Holy Spirit. Because the Creator wills and loves the creation, because Yahweh loves and forgives Israel, we recognize God is vulnerable and God suffers. The cross is the final and ultimate event in God and in the world of the suffering and victorious love of Yahweh, the Eternal Trinity. This means that whenever "Father" is used of Yahweh in the Scriptures of Israel, we must think of it as an "image" for God, not the "person" of the Trinity whom Jesus addresses as *abba*. It refers to God's vulnerable and suffering love. Ultimately, then, our retrieval of the event of the cross means that whenever we say "God" to refer to the "Father" of Jesus, the "Son," then we must think or say: God the Father, that "person" of the Holy Trinity to whom Jesus, the Son, referred to as "Father."

The "Son" reveals "Father" as Creator and world as creation. We could say many things about God as creator. Here, we will simply recognize that it is Jesus who addresses the One whose mission he shares as *abba*. It is an intimate familial form of speaking to God—which, although not entirely unique to Jesus, is nevertheless not typical in Israel. As such, this use of language discloses the identity within God as the One to whom Jesus relates as "Son."

The characteristic of the One whom Jesus calls *abba* is the suffering love which gives the Son into alienation and death (Romans 8:31-32; John 3:16), and thus shares the experience of alienation and death in this distinct way.

The world was already confessed as creation in Israel. The early creed in Deuteronomy 26:5-10 begins by identifying Abraham as the "wandering Aramean," to whom God delivered a promise of nationhood ("I will make of you a great nation"). The period of tribal confederacy which followed was a struggle for community. The later creed in Nehemiah 9:6-38 opens by recognizing the Lord as creator with the words, "You alone; you have made heaven." The point is that Israel is thinking about its origins not only as a community of people with shared ancestry, but more—as a people chosen by a particular God. *This* God, the One who is *creator*.

With God as creator, the world is identified as creation. To be creation means that the world is intended and wanted, that it is good, that it has a positive destiny, that it is to be received in faith and thanksgiving, and finally, that it is to be affirmed and loved. Initially, the doctrine of creation is a statement of vision: It is about how one looks at the world, regards the world, treats the world—and all of this based on the Gospel. It is derivatively a confession of the world's ultimate origin (creation) and destiny (the new creation that is the consummation of the reign of God).

The confession that the world is made *ex nihilo*, "from nothing," is a confession of the world's contingency—that it is not necessary, that it is the consequence of God's gift and grace and love. The grounding for such recognition and confession is the resurrection of Jesus the Messiah from the nothingness of death. Hence Jesus' resurrection, as the ultimate affirmation of life, is the grounding for both the confession of creation and the confession of new creation. O'Donovan is instructive here:

> In proclaiming the resurrection of Christ, the apostles proclaimed also the resurrection of humankind in Christ; and in proclaiming the resurrection of humankind, they proclaimed the renewal of all creation with him. The resurrection of Christ in isolation from humankind would not be a Gospel message. The resurrection of humankind apart from creation would be a Gospel of a sort, but of a purely gnostic and world-denying sort which is far from the Gospel that the apostles actually preached. So the resurrection of Christ directs our attention back to the creation which it vindicates.

But we must understand "creation" not merely as the raw material out of which the world as we know it is composed, but as the order and coherence *in* which it is composed. To speak of the resurrection of creation would be meaningless if creation were no more than so much undifferentiated energy. Such a proclamation can have point only as it assures us that the very thing which God has made will continue and flourish. It is not created energy as such that is vindicated in the resurrection of Christ, but the order in which created energy was disposed by the hand of the Creator.[238]

So in the eschaton, when all creation is the final and full object of God's redemptive reign, we will recognize salvation as God's doing and gift in Jesus, the Messiah. We understand that the world as creation is the gift of the Father because the Father loves the Son, for the love of the Father that is revealed in the Son is not self-absorbing, but self-offering. Therefore, the world is distinct from and other than God, an act of the utter freedom of the Triune God to offer from God to creation its very existence. Here we recognize again how God's *actions* reveal the *beingness* of God: For it is an act of voluntary openness to vulnerability, openness to the claims of that which is other than the Triune God, openness to suffering love.

The world is the creation of the Father, through the Son, animated by the life-giving power and quality of the Holy Spirit. As Jenson tells us:

The being of the triune God is a great Conversation, and creation happens in that the Father, Son, and Spirit mention among themselves others than themselves, so that these others must be. Now we add: there are creatures whose creatureliness we specify as "humanity," in that Father, Son, and Spirit also take some creatures *into* the Conversation, in that God addresses *homo sapiens* and waits for an answer.[239]

The Son confers the Holy Spirit as the Spirit in which we see the victory of life over the powers of death and sin. Recall that we might want to understand the Holy Spirit as the "down payment" on the eschaton, the power and presence of the eschatological reign of God already here and now in the midst of the continuing power and presence of the reign of death and sin.

In the final outcome of history, the Holy Spirit is the Spirit of authentic freedom *for* the world, not from the world. The Holy Spirit is the Spirit of love and laughter, of peace and joy, of hope and possibility. The Holy Spirit is the subject of glorifying the Father and the Son, and thus unifying the Father and the Son. Thus, the Holy Spirit is the subject and author of unity, unifying the Father and the Son, unifying humanity, unifying humanity with the rest of creation. As Moltmann says, "The personhood of God the Holy Spirit is the loving, self-communicating, out-spreading and out-pouring presence of the eternal divine life of the triune God."[240]

The Suffering of God

That the cross of Jesus is something that happens to God raises anew the question of the suffering of God. As mentioned, patripassianism (the idea that it was the Father who suffered on the cross) was condemned as heretical in the second century because it was a form of modalism.[241] The theopaschites of the sixth century were condemned because of their claim that Jesus had only one nature—the divine nature, which thus denied Jesus' humanity.

The Jewish confession of God gives the *events* of history priority over claims made about the *beingness* of God. God is defined by active involvement in history. By looking to history, we can say that God is whoever delivered Israel from bondage, preserves its life in the wilderness, gives it both victory and defeat. God elects Israel and gives Israel both conditional and eschatological promise. Because Israel confesses God's involvement in history, Israel also confesses God's freedom to suffer. God suffers because God loves Israel.

Unlike the ancient Greeks who often thought of the universe as an unintended emanation, the Jews confessed the world as creation because they believed that God wanted the world. But that very confession leads to two astonishingly bold assertions. The first bold assertion is that by creating a world which is not God, God engaged in a free act of self-limitation. God's freedom is such that God can willingly and joyfully limit and condition that freedom. There is now something (creation) over against God, something which God wants to take into account. The second bold assertion is that by wanting a world and wanting to take that world into account, God becomes vulnerable. Like lovers in a marriage, like the parents of children, God becomes vulnerable because God loves the "other" which God has called into existence.

This, it seems to me, is the Jewish—and Christian—way to address the problem of evil in the world. Love and vulnerability and suffering go hand in hand. We suffer when those whom we love suffer, and especially when we are helpless in the face of their suffering. We can also suffer at the hands of those whom we love. And we can suffer on behalf of those whom we love. The scriptures of Israel proclaim that God experiences such vulnerable and suffering love in all three ways.

The cross of Jesus is the ultimate event in which suffering unto death itself becomes an experience in the history of God. But just such suffering unto death requires at least the beginning of the confession of God as Trinity—that is, the confession of the Father and the Son. We experience death in two ways: in our own death and in the death of those we love. The Son suffers by dying the humiliating death of the slave (Philippians 2:8), and the Father suffers by giving the Son over to the God-forsakenness of the cross (Mark 15:34; Romans 8:31-32). The doctrine of the Trinity proclaims that God the Father and God the Son suffer in the world, with the world, at the hands of the world, on behalf of the world in the cross. There is now no place so lonely or tormented where God is not in solidarity with suffering (Romans 8:33-39).

The Meaning of the Oneness of God

The oneness of God is not the oneness of a single unit (which would imply that God is one in a series), but rather the oneness of absolute or ultimate singularity, the oneness of uniqueness. Ultimacy is singular or it is not ultimate. God alone is God, and no thing or no other is God. That is the meaning of Israel's great *Shema Yisrael Adonai elochenu*

Adonai echad: "Hear, O Israel, The Lord our God, the Lord is One" (Deuteronomy 6:4).[242]

The singularity or uniqueness of the God experienced in the history of Israel and its Messiah, Jesus, is that God is forgiving, saving, merciful through compassion—literally, "suffering with" (Hosea 11:8-9; Romans 11:33-36; Matthew 20:1-16). Hence, the oneness of God is evangelical, a unique claim of the Gospel.

However, also in Jewish thought distinct identities can be identified within the singularity of God. "Perfection" or "holiness" for Israel or for disciples of Jesus means being "set apart" for God's purposes, for purposes of the reign of God. "Perfection" or "holiness" as descriptive of God means God's uniqueness—that which distinguishes God from sinful humanity. The biblical vision of God's kind of holiness (God's unique "perfection") is that God is involved with the world as one who suffers and who redeems through suffering with and for the world. The Christian claim is that God's suffering is ultimately grounded in the crucifixion of Jesus. That is, therefore, in Christian terms, the basis for confessing God as Trinity.

Some Implications for the Christian Life

The claims I am making thus far lead me to underscore the necessity and the importance of the doctrine of the Trinity by identifying some of its implications for the Christian life.

- The doctrine of the Trinity identifies the God of the Gospel, namely, Jesus, the Messiah and the Son of God, his Father, and the Holy Spirit who is Lord of the eschatological future created by the suffering and victorious love of the Father and the Son. To confess their unity, to confess the three as one God, is to confess the singularity of God. There is no other god because there is no other Gospel. This God— Father, Son, and Holy Spirit—constitutes a life and mission into which we are entered and within which we will find our final destiny. That is what it means to affirm the doctrine of the Trinity.

- The God of the Gospel—Father, Son, Holy Spirit—is world affirming. That is the implication of confessing this God—Father, Son, Holy Spirit—as creator and preserver of the world. Therefore those who trust/hope in this God— Father, Son, Holy Spirit—receive the world as gift, enjoy its pleasures and arrangements, seek to live in harmony with it, and accept humanity's calling to be steward of creation.

- The God of the Gospel—Father, Son, Holy Spirit—creates and calls the messianic community, the church, to be a community of anticipation, a community which is called to embody the vision of peace and justice which characterizes the reign of God. Indeed, the church has authority in the midst of a fallen humanity because it embodies God's future for all, for women as well as men, for young and old, for poor and affluent, for weak and strong, for oppressed and oppressor. Just as Jesus' authority came from promise, not precedent, so the messianic community at Pentecost received the Spirit by which both women and men would exercise prophetic leadership, not to predict the future, but to announce and embody God's future. This is the context in which the church must address the question of the ordained ministry of women. This is the context in which the church must address questions of peace and justice.

- The God of the Gospel—Father, Son, Holy Spirit—calls the messianic community which is the church to be catholic, that is, both universal and orthodox. The call to be universal means that the church is home to all races and nations, to all sorts and conditions of humanity where "there is no longer Greek and Jew, circumcised and uncircumcised, barbarian, Scythian, slave and free; but Christ is all and in all" (Colossians 3: 9-11). Orthodoxy does not mean correct ideology. It means attention to the church's Gospel so that its witness and its praise are authentic. The authentic good news of the church is this: Jesus is risen! Orthodoxy asks what this good news means for the witness of the church in its worship and polity, in its teaching and life.

- The God of the Gospel—Father, Son, Holy Spirit—is liberating. If death has the last word, then the only thing to do is to preserve ourselves at the expense of others. But if Jesus is risen and the reign of God has the last word, then there is more to life than preserving it. Hence the ultimate witness (*martyria*) is the freedom to resist every tyranny and oppression, to be in solidarity with victims even at the cost of our lives. If we fear for our lives, we will never be free. Hence the words of Jesus: "Those who want to save their life will lose it (anyway), and those who lose their life for my sake, and for the sake of the Gospel, will save it" (Mark 8:35).

- The God of the Gospel—Father, Son, Holy Spirit—is the compassionate God who suffers in solidarity with the suffering. The messianic community which is the church is therefore called to enter into solidarity with all those who suffer. The church is called to care for victims of evil, illness, and disaster, and thus to witness to the compassionate God of the Gospel—Father, Son, Holy Spirit.

- The God of the Gospel—Father, Son, Holy Spirit—is the God of new possibilities, that is, the God of forgiveness of sins. Therefore, the messianic community which is the church is called to forgive enemies, to create new possibilities for friend and foe alike.

When Paul contemplates the God of the Gospel, he bursts into praise: "Oh, the depth of the riches and wisdom and knowledge of God! How unsearchable are his judgments and how inscrutable his ways!" (Romans 11:33-34). And in so saying, Paul is thinking about God's mercy—to Israel and to the Gentile world. That is God's singularity, God's oneness.

That is also God's mystery: For the mystery is *not* what God is in God's *being*. That is disclosed in the Gospel: God is Jesus, crucified and risen, his Father, and the Spirit of the final future.

Nor is the mystery in what God *does*: God creates, suffers, promises. In short, God loves.

The mystery is *why* God *bothers*, *why* God *loves*, *why* God is *merciful*.

God does bother with us and with our world. Perhaps someday we will know why. But if we never find out, it will not matter.

ENDNOTES

1   John Updike, *Telephone Poles and Other Poems*, 1st ed. (New York: Alfred A. Knopf, 1963), 72-73.

2   Gerald O'Collins' overview of non-Christian counter explanations of the crucifixion and resurrection of Jesus is instructive here. See G. S. J. O'Collins, *Jesus Risen: An Historical, Fundamental and Systematic Examination of Christ's Resurrection* (New York: Paulist Press, 1987).

3   Wolfhart Pannenberg, *An Introduction to Systematic Theology* (Grand Rapids: Wm. B. Eerdmans Publishing Company, 1991).

4   Hans Von Campenhausen, "The Events of Easter and the Empty Tomb," in *Tradition and Life in the Church*.

5   To say that we live in "post-modern pluralist religiosity" is to recognize that unlike pre-Enlightenment years, no longer does only one worldview prevail. Instead, many conflicting claims compete for our attention and commitment. Philosopher Jean-Francois Lyotard (1924-1998) promoted the post-modern worldview. His incredulous attitude toward "grand narratives" was meant to assert the death of the community's overarching, meaningful story. Disappearance of a grand narrative from the larger culture calls into question the very possibility of objective truth, thereby reducing religion to individualistic private meanings—if, indeed, there is even any such thing as "meaning." Secondly, post-modernism purports a "de-centering" of perspective, along with the discovery of "otherness," "difference," and "marginality" as valid modes of approach to experience. These two features (the rejection of grand narratives and the de-centering of perspective) are related to one another, since it is the rejection of unitary narratives and justifications that open the way to an acceptance of plurality and difference. Since there is no objective narrative at all, Christianity cannot argue over whether or not competing narratives are true or false; that is, there is nothing to argue with, for as no one claims a perspective, there is no one with whom to have a meaningful conversation.

6   C.S. Lewis, *Beyond Personality: The Christian Idea of God* (New York: The Macmillan Co., 1945).

7   During the 1930s and 1940s, German Nazis promoted a revised form of Christianity called *Deutsches Christentum*, in which they replaced the Old Testament with Germanic myths and legends. Although *Deutsches Christentum* did not achieve public acceptance, its anti-Semitic origins characterized the thinking of the Nazi party, and contributed to the martyrdom of numerous German Christians.

8   Editor's note: This reference is from an article written by Dr. Bouman follow-ing his cancer diagnosis. Walter R. Bouman, "Faith Sustains and Comforts as End of This Life Draws Near," *The Columbus Dispatch*, June 17, 2005.

9   N. T. Wright, *The Challenge of Jesus: Rediscovering Who Jesus Was and Is* (Downers Grove, Illinois: InterVarsity Press, 1999).

10 Pinchas Lapide, *The Resurrection of Jesus: A Jewish Perspective* (Minneapolis: Augsburg Publishing House, 1983).

11 Also see Romans 1:1-4, Romans 10:9, and Galatians 1:1.

12 Mark Allan Powell, *Fortress Introduction to the Gospels* (Minneapolis: Augsburg Fortress, 1998).

13 Robert H. Smith, *The Easter Gospels: The Resurrection of Jesus According to the Four Evangelists* (Minneapolis: Augsburg Publishing House, 1983).

14 Powell, *Fortress Introduction to the Gospels.*

15 Ibid., 2.

16 Robert Smith, *Easter Gospels* (Minneapolis: Augsburg Publishing House, 1983).

17 Powell, *Fortress Introduction to the Gospels.*

18 Smith, *The Easter Gospels: The Resurrection of Jesus According to the Four Evangelists.*

19 Powell, *Fortress Introduction to the Gospels.*

20 Lapide, *The Resurrection of Jesus: A Jewish Perspective.*

21 Günther Bornkamm, *The New Testament: A Guide to Its Writings* (Philadelphia: Fortress Press, 1973).

22 Immanuel Kant, "Critique of Pure Reason," in *The Cambridge Edition of the Works of Immanuel Kant*, ed. Paul Guyer and Allen W. Wood (New York: Cambridge University Press, 1999).

23 Apocalyptic literature was written or used by the people of Israel during times of intense persecution and suffering. It must be understood as "code language." It looks for dramatic divine intervention in history in which the persecutors are defeated, and the victims are vindicated. "Signs" suggest that the dramatic divine intervention is about to occur, or will enable victims to recognize when it is about to occur. Biblical examples are Daniel, Revelation, Mark 13, Matthew 24 and 25, and Luke 21.

24 To call the four accounts of the resurrection "traditions" is to recognize that the authors are thought to have inherited these portions of their Gospels from an earlier source. Powell, *Fortress Introduction to the Gospels*, 173.

25 James D. G. Dunn, *The Evidence for Jesus* (Louisville: The Westminster Press, 1985).

26 N. T. Wright, *The Resurrection of the Son of God*, 5 vols., vol. 3, Christian Origins and the Question of God (Minneapolis: Fortress Press, 2003).

27 Wright, *The Challenge of Jesus: Rediscovering Who Jesus Was and Is.*

28 Ibid.

29 ———, *The Resurrection of the Son of God*.

30 Acts 4:11-12.

31 Acts 3:6.

32 Acts 7:59; 1 Corinthians 1:2; 2 Corinthians 12:8.

33 Philippians 2:6-11; 1 Timothy 2:5-6; 3:16.

34 Revelation 5:9-10. See also the summary by Martin Hengel: "1) Liturgical hymns had a special significance in the meetings for worship of the earliest Christian mission communities, and were an essential part of that worship. 2) These were not just traditional songs; they will just as often have been spontaneous compositions. They were not regarded as purely human creations, but as works of the Holy Spirit. 3) In content the liturgical hymn was primarily governed by the saving event which had been brought about in Christ, i.e., it was predominantly a hymn to Christ. 4) Despite the variety of possibilities, in form it will have been a 'psalm.'" Martin Hengel, *Between Jesus and Paul: Studies in the Earliest History of Christianity* (Eugene, Oregon: Wipf & Stock Publishers, 2003).

35 Acts 8:16.

36 Mark Allan Powell disputed this translation of the text with one of the interpreters of the New Revised Standard Version of the Bible, and pointed out that the original documents say that "When they saw him, they worshiped him, but doubted." The interpreter conceded the point. The correction strengthens the points being made here.

37 Dunn, *The Evidence for Jesus*, 70.

38 Jürgen Moltmann, *Theology of Hope: On the Ground and the Implications of a Christian Eschatology* (Minneapolis: Fortress Press, 1993), 165-66.

39 Ibid.

40 Romans 1:1-7.

41 To say that Paul's epistle is grounding for the assertion of justification by faith is to recognize that we are made righteous before God through our faith or acceptance of Jesus as Lord.

42 Theology of the cross, also called "theology from below," is an expression which varies somewhat with its usage. For Werner Elert (*The Christian Faith*, 1940) it means that the person and the work of Christ belong inseparably together, that "christology" means "soteriology," that what Jesus Christ does determines what Jesus Christ is. Wolfhart Pannenberg (*Jesus—God and Man*, 1968) uses the phrase to identify a method which begins with the history of Jesus and moves forward to the confession of his divinity. "Christology from below" carries with it the problem that one is starting with a Platonic or "ontological" framework, but reversing it. The method employed by Pannenberg is, in fact, too complex to be described by this phrase. This systematic theology approaches christology from the perspective of history, as will be shown in Chapter 2.

43 N.T. Wright, *The Challenge of Jesus: Rediscovering Who Jesus Was and Is* (Downers Grove, Illinois: InterVarsity Press, 1999), 146-47.

44 Wright, *The Resurrection of the Son of God*, 736.

45 N.T. Wright, *The New Testament and the People of God*, 5 vols., vol. 1, Christian Origins and the Question of God (Minneapolis: Fortress Press, 1992), 333.

46 "The universe has two possible destinies. It may continue to expand forever, or it may recollapse and come to an end at the big crunch. I predict the universe in time will come to an end at the big crunch. I do, however, have certain advantages over other prophets of doom. Whatever happens ten billion years from now, I don't expect to be around to be proved wrong." Stephen Hawking, *A Brief History of Time: A Reader's Companion* (New York: Bantam, 1992).

47 Wolfhart Pannenberg, *Theology and the Kingdom of God* (Philadelphia: Westminster John Knox Press, 1969), 56.

48 Acts 10:42b. Also see 1 Corinthians 15:24-28, 42-57 and Ephesians 1:17-23.

49 2 Corinthians 1:18-19.

50 Ultimately, christology also must deal with the church's *lex docendi*, or teaching, about Christ—which eventually was summarized by the dogma that the Second Person of the Holy Trinity is understood as having two natures: human and divine. This aspect of christology will be addressed in later chapters.

51 Carl Braaten, "Locus 6," in *Christian Dogmatics* (1984).

52 Jürgen Moltmann, *The Way of Jesus Christ* (1989).

53 Wright, *The Challenge of Jesus: Rediscovering Who Jesus Was and Is*, 102.

54 "Between the Babylonian destruction of the first Jerusalem temple (587/6 B.C.E.) and the Roman destruction of the second Jerusalem temple (70 C.E.) were created the formative elements of Judaism as a major religious system. These two demolitions focus attention on the centrality of the Jerusalem temple for the period and emphasize the importance of outside imperial powers in determining the shape of Jewish religion." Robert P. Carroll, "Israel, History of (Post-Monarchic Period)," in *Anchor Bible Dictionary*, ed. David Noel Freedman (New York: Doubleday, 1992), 567.

55 YHWH refers to Yahweh, the name of God, which is not to be spoken or written, according to Ancient Judaism.

56 Ezekiel 1 and Daniel 7 point to, wonder about and offer possibilities for characteristics of the one who would be God's agent. Other texts—particularly Isaiah 40 to 55—further develop the idea that God will again act in the history of the world.

57 Wright, *The Challenge of Jesus: Rediscovering Who Jesus Was and Is*, 105.

58 Throughout its history, Israel was surrounded by nations who venerated a variety of other gods. The texts of Second Isaiah (primarily Isaiah 40–55), however, reveal Israel's assertion of monotheism—or worship of the Lord as the One True God: the One who was revealed in the Exodus, and who is known through promise and fulfillment. Moreover, not only was the Lord the

only deity; the texts also claim that the Lord was the god of all peoples. As such, Israel was admonished to be "light to the nations," carrying the truth of the Lord to all peoples. Monotheists, then, allowed that there is only one god: the Lord. Such an understanding does not limit their understanding of who-God-is. Indeed, Jewish understanding of monotheism was applied in the first century to the assertion that Jesus the Christ (the One who is beyond death) is God.

59   Wright, *The Challenge of Jesus: Rediscovering Who Jesus Was and Is,* 105.

60   ———, *The Resurrection of the Son of God,* 726.

61   Ibid.

62   Ibid., 733.

63   Cf. Romans 8:29; Colossians 1:18; and Hebrews 12:22-24.

64   Cf. Matthew 28:19-20, Acts 10:9-48, Acts 15:12-18, Acts 28:28, Romans 1:5, and Romans 11:11-16.

65   Acts 10:42b. Also see 1 Corinthians 15:24-28, 42-57, and Ephesians 1:17-23.

66   Pannenberg, *Theology and the Kingdom of God,* 60.

67   "Sinner" is used in a factional context to denote persons outside the boundary of the group. An obvious example of this use is when "sinner" is seen as a synonym for "Gentile." In the Gospels, see Matthew 5:47, Mark 14:41, Luke 6:33, as well as other texts. James D. G. Dunn says, "In such passages the unifying concept is not that Gentiles are by definition murderers and robbers. Rather it is that their conduct lay outside the boundary of the law. They were literally lawless: They did not have the law because they did not belong to the covenant people, the people of the law. And so, not knowing the torah, naturally they did not keep it." James D.G. Dunn, "Pharisees, Sinners, and Jesus," in *The Social World of Formative Christianity and Judaism: Essays in Tribute to Howard Clark Kee,* ed. Richard Horsley (Philadelphia: Fortress Press, 1988), 276.

68   Greek concepts of "god" can be traced to the Milesian school of philosophy which was brought into existence by Greek contact with Babylonians and Egyptians. Anaximander, the second philosopher of this school in about 610 B.C., posited the origin of creation from a single, primal substance that is *infinite, eternal* and *ageless* and "encompasses all the worlds." The attributes of this so-called "primal substance" provided the basis for Greek characteristics of the deity. Bertrand Russell, *A History of Western Philosophy* (New York: Simon & Schuster, 1972).

69   Judy Pearsall and Bill Trumble, eds., *The Oxford Encyclopedic English Dictionary,* 2nd ed. (New York: Oxford University Press, 1995).

70   Robert W. Jenson, "The Triune God," in *Christian Dogmatics,* ed. Carl E. Braaten (Philadelphia: Fortress Press, 1984).

71   It is useful to note here that Kant's *Critique of Pure Reason,* mentioned in chapter 1, radically called into question all philosophy and theology whose epistemology (or theory of knowing) was based on the arguments for the

existence of a supernatural idea of god—that is, a god defined in Hellenistic terms: a god for whom no sense data was available.

72   Emanation refers to an ancient Greek theory about the origin of the world as a process in which a series of hierarchically descending radiations move from a divine source, or deity, through various intermediate stages until ultimately becoming matter.

73   Use of the title *"Logos"* in the Gospel of John functions to name Jesus as God. In John 1, the *Logos* which "becomes flesh and lived among us" (v. 14) is simply given the title "God." And in John 20:28, Thomas calls the risen Jesus, "My Lord and my God!"

74   Here, "Being" refers to *homoousios*.

75   Echoes of John 1:3, "All things came into being through him, and without him not one thing came into being," which was written at the end of the first century, can be heard in this creed. The classic Hellenistic "work" of the *Logos* is reflected in this passage.

76   Likewise at Nicaea, Athanasius (296-373 A.D.) had insisted that if the *Logos* did not take on the entire human nature, then humanity could not be redeemed, for from his point of view—a Greek interpretation of god—whatever was not assumed by the *Logos* would not be redeemed.

77   Examples include Socinianism, liberalism, Unitarianism, and secularism.

78   See Isobel Carter Heyward, *The Redemption of God* (University Press of America, 1982).

79   Robert Farrar Capon, *Hunting the Divine Fox: Images and Mystery in Christian Faith* (New York: The Seabury Press, 1974), 90-92.

80   N.T. Wright concurs with the misleading nature of the Superman myth, asserting that it is "ultimately a dualistic corruption of the Christian story." Wright, *The Challenge of Jesus: Rediscovering Who Jesus Was and Is*, 15.

81   *Dr. Martin Luther's Large Catechism*, trans. J. N. Lenker (Minneapolis: Augsburg Publishing House, 1935).

82   Paul Tillich, *Dynamics of Faith* (New York: Harper & Row, Publishers, Inc., 1957).

83   Güenther Bornkamm, *Jesus of Nazareth*, trans. Irene and Fraser McLuskey with James M. Robinson (New York: Harper & Row, Publishers, 1960), 23. Cf. John 1:18: "No one has ever seen God. It is God the only Son, who is close to the Father's heart, who has made him known."

84   Romans 6:9.

85   Early in my teaching career, I used the phrase "kingdom of God" to express the ideas in this section. I changed the phrase to "reign of God" because the word "kingdom" contains the word "king" and as such, leads to a decidedly *un*intentional masculine inference. To avoid the gender issue, "reign of God" is a more accurate use of language.

86 Garry Wills, *Lincoln at Gettysburg: The Words That Remade America* (New York: Touchtone, 1992).

87 The "event of Jesus" refers to the life, crucifixion, and resurrection of Jesus and what these occurrences mean.

88 Dante Alighieri, *Divine Comedy: Inferno, Purgatory, Paradise*, vol. Canto XXXIII (New York: Everyman's Library, 1995).

89 Stanley Hauerwas, *Truthfulness and Tragedy: Further Investigations into Christian Ethics* (South Bend, Indiana: University of Notre Dame Press, 1977).

90 Ibid.

91 N.T. Wright, *Jesus and the Victory of God*, 5 vols., vol. 2, Christian Origins and the Question of God (Minneapolis: Fortress Press, 1996), 530, with n. 186

92 Ibid., 231.

93 Daniel 2:31-35: "You were looking, O king, and lo! There was a great statue. This statue was huge, its brilliance extraordinary; it was standing before you, and its appearance was frightening. The head of that statue was of fine gold, its chest and arms of silver, its middle and thighs of bronze, its legs of iron. Its feet partly of iron and partly of clay. As you looked on, a stone was cut out, not by human hands, and it struck the statue on its feet of iron and clay and broke them in pieces. Then the iron, the clay, the bronze, the silver, and the gold, were all broken in pieces and became like the chaff of the summer threshing floors; and the wind carried them away, so that not a trace of them could be found. But the stone that struck the statue became a great mountain and filled the whole earth."

94 Wright, *Jesus and the Victory of God*, 5.

95 The italics are from the original text. Arland J. Hultgren, *Christ and His Benefits: Christology and Redemption in the New Testament* (Philadelphia: Fortress Press, 1987), 187-88.

96 Matthew 11:2-6.

97 Matthew 12:27.

98 Jürgen Moltmann, *The Way of Jesus Christ: Christology in Messianic Dimensions*, trans. Margaret Kohl (New York: HarperCollins Publishers, 1990), 108-09.

99 Luke 15:1-2; Luke 19:1-10

100 George Arthur Buttrick, ed., *Psalms of Solomon*, 4 vols. vol. 3, The Interpreter's Dictionary of the Bible (Nashville: Abingdon Press, 1962).

101 See Matthew 5–7. Matthew can be read in two ways. One is to understand that the whole Gospel is new torah; and that it is divided into five sections, corresponding to Genesis, Exodus, Leviticus, Numbers, Deuteronomy. Another is to say that it is even smaller than that, and maybe more beautifully crafted than that, and in this interpretation we would say that Matthew puts together the Sermon on the Mount (also called the Beatitudes) as new torah.

102 Deuteronomy 30:15-20.

103 Bornkamm, *Jesus of Nazareth*, 23.

104 Joachim Jeremias, *The Parables of Jesus*, trans. S. H. Hooke (New York: SCM Press Ltd., 1963), 138.

105 Eric Berne, *What Do You Say after Hello?* (New York: Bantam Books, 1973).

106 John Dominic Crossan, *The Dark Interval: Toward a Theology of Story*, 121.

107 Matthew 22:1-10; Luke 14:16-24.

108 Luke 15:3-7.

109 Luke 15:8-10.

110 Luke 15:11-32.

111 See also Luke 10:25-37 or Matthew 18:23-35.

112 Martin Hengel, *Crucifixion* (Philadelphia: Fortress Press, 1977).

113 Hultgren, *Christ and His Benefits: Christology and Redemption in the New Testament*, 31-32.

114 Wright, *The Challenge of Jesus: Rediscovering Who Jesus Was and Is*.

115 Ibid.

116 Jürgen Moltmann, *The Crucified God*, trans. R.A. Wilson and John Bowden, 1st U.S. ed. (New York: SCM Press Ltd., 1974).

117 Günther Bornkamm (*Jesus of Nazareth*), Ernst Käsemann (*Jesus Means Freedom*), and Gerhardt Forde (*Christian Dogmatics, Locus 7*) agree with Moltmann's interpretation.

118 Wright, *The Challenge of Jesus: Rediscovering Who Jesus Was and Is*.

119 Ibid.

120 Moltmann, *The Crucified God*.

121 Wright, *The Challenge of Jesus: Rediscovering Who Jesus Was and Is*.

122 Martin Hengel, *Crucifixion*.

123 John 18:1, Matthew 26:36, Mark 14:32, Luke 22:39.

124 Questions have been raised whether this is a reference to topography or to the fact that bones (and skulls) littered the place of execution because many of those who were executed were not buried.

125 Also note the importance of drinking in John 4:7, 9, 10; 6:53, 55; 7:37, and 18:11.

126 Also see Acts 4:10-11; Acts 7:52; Acts 10:39; Acts 13:28, etc.

127 Hengel, *Crucifixion*.

128 ———, *Crucifixion*.

129 Galatians 3:13.

130 Forde, *Christian Dogmatics*.

131 *The Loci Communes of Philipp Melanchthon*, trans. Charles L. Hill (Boston: Meador Publishing Co., 1944).

132 Arland J. Hultgren, *Christ and His Benefits: Christology and Redemption in the New Testament* (Philadelphia: Fortress Press, 1987).

133 Italics added. Gerhard Forde, *Theology Is for Proclamation* (Minneapolis: Augsburg Fortress, 1990).

134 H. J. Iwand, *"Christologievollesung"* (unpublished). Moltmann, *The Crucified God*.

135 Translation for *sola fide* is "only by faith," and *opera Dei* is the "works of God."

136 Gustaf Aulén, *Christus Victor: An Historical Study of the Three Main Types of Atonement*, trans. A. G. Hebert (London: SPCK, 1950).

137 Proponents of this approach are Gustaf Aulén and theologians of the ancient church such as Irenaeus, Athanasius, and Gregory of Nyssa. Paul's epistle to the Romans (8:31-39) and Martin Luther's *Mighty Fortress is Our God* also use battlefield language.

138 Venantius Honorius Fortunatus, "Welcome, Happy Morning," in *Lutheran Book of Worship* (Minneapolis: Augsburg Publishing House, 1996).

139 Irenaeus, *Irenaeus against Heresies* (Whitefish, Montana: Kessinger Publishing, 2004).

140 "But if it is by the Spirit of God that I cast our demons, then the kingdom of God has come to you. Or how can one enter a strong man's house and plunder his property, without first tying up the strong man? Then indeed the house can be plundered."

141 John 8:44: You are from your father the devil, and you choose to do your father's desires. He was a murderer from the beginning and does not stand in the truth, because there is no truth in him. When he lies, he speaks according to his own nature, for he is a liar and the father of lies.

142 Irenaeus, *Irenaeus against Heresies*.

143 Athanasius, *The Incarnation of the Word of God* (New York: Macmillan, 1954).

144 Gregory of Nyssa, *The Great Cathechism*

145 See, for example, Genesis 3, John 8:44; Matthew 12:29; Colossians 2:15; Hebrews 2:14-18.

146 Johann Heermann, "Ah, Holy Jesus," in *Lutheran Book of Worship* (Minneapolis: Augsburg Publishing House, 1978).

147 Donnie McClurkin, "Lord, I Lift Your Name on High," in *Live in London and More* (2000).

148 Anselm of Canterbury (1033-1109), *Cur Deus Homo.*

149 See, for example, 1 Timothy 2:6; Revelation 5:9; John 1:29 and 36; 1 Corinthians 5:7; and 1 Peter 1:19.

150 Frances R. Havergal, "Lord, Speak to Us, That We May Speak " in *Lutheran Book of Worship* (Minneapolis: Augsburg Publishing House, 1978).

151 Peter Abelard, "Exposition of the Epistle to the Romans," in *A Scholastic Miscellany: Anselm to Ockham* (Philadelphia: The Westminster Press, 1956).

152 John 15:13.

153 John Masius, in *Touched by an Angel* (U.S.: 20th Century Fox, 1994).

154 Frank Capra, "It's a Wonderful Life," (U.S.: Liberty Films (II), 1947).

155 Gerhard O. Forde, "The Work of Christ," in *Christian Dogmatics*, ed. Carl E. Braaten and Robert W. Jenson (Philadelphia: Fortress Press, 1984).

156 Also see Galatians 2:20, Ephesians 5:2 and 25; Titus 2:14, and Timothy 2:6.

157 Helmut Gollwitzer, *The Dying and Living Lord* (Philadelphia: Muhlenberg Press 1960).

158 2 Corinthians 5:17.

159 Forde, "The Work of Christ."

160 ———, *Theology Is for Proclamation*.

161 Romans 6:1-11.

162 Romans 9:5, cf. Philippians 2:6.

163 Thomas C. Oden, *The Structure of Awareness* (Nashville: Abingdon Press, 1969).

164 When reviewing this text, Luke Bouman offered here a theological critique provided by his father, Walter Bouman: He also recognized that this perspective is a perceived challenge of the industrialized or Western world, and that the challenge of the developing world in the present is survival, not meaning.

165 Douglas John Hall, *Lighten Our Darkness: Toward an Indigenous Theology of the Cross* (Philadelphia: The Westminster Press, 1976).

166 The comments here are from a 1993 lecture, and therefore reflect early warnings about environmental hazards and global warming.

167 Hannah Arendt, *On Revolution*, 10th ed. (New York: The Viking Press, Inc., 1970).

168 The quote is actually, "It's not true that life is one damn thing after another—it's one damn thing over and over..." From a letter penned by Edna St. Vincent Millay to Arthur Davison Ficke on October 24, 1930. Allan Ross Macdougall, ed., *Letters of Edna St. Vincent Millay* (New York: Harper & Brothers, Publishers, 1952), 240.

169 Ephesians 1:17-18.

170 Moltmann, *The Way of Jesus Christ*.

171 Cf. the meaning of nudity in Genesis 2:25: "And the man and his wife were both naked, and were not ashamed."

172 Helmut Thielicke, *Death and Life*, trans. Edward H. Schroeder (Philadelphia: Fortress Press, 1970).

173 Harold Bloom, *The American Religion: The Re-Emergence of the Post-Christian Nation* (New York: Simon & Schuster, 1993)

174 Edgar Lee Masters, *Spoon River Anthology* (New York: The Macmillan Company, 1915).

175 See also Krister Stendahl, ed., *Immortality and Resurrection* (New York: Macmillan, 1965), especially the essay by Oscar Cullman in which he points out the distinction between the Christian confession and the Greek expectation.

176 Robert Farrar Capon, *Kingdom, Grace, Judgment: Paradox, Outrage, and Vindication in the Parables of Jesus*, Combined Ed. (Grand Rapids: Wm. B. Eerdmans Publishing Company, 2002).

177 Hans Schwarz, *Eschatology* (Grand Rapids: Wm. B. Eerdmans Publishing Company, 2001). Cf. *On the Way to the Future: A Christian View of Eschatology in the Light of Current Trends in Religion, Philosophy, and Science* (Minneapolis: Augsburg Publishing, 1972).

178 Ascension narratives supporting this worldview can be found in Luke 24:50-53 and Acts 1:6-11. Also see Luke 16:19-31; Matthew 25:31-46; 1 Thessalonians 4:13-18.

179 Lewis, *The Great Divorce*, 126-127.

180 Robert W. Jenson, "How the World Lost Its Story," *First Things* (1993).

181 Matthew 5:22-30.

182 Luke 16:19-31

183 Robert W. Jenson, "The Last Judgment," *Ad Fontes*.

184 Darrell J. Fasching, *The Coming of the Millennium: Good News for the Whole Human Race* (Lincoln, Nebraska: Authors Choice Press, 2001).

185 Robert Farrar Capon, *The Foolishness of Preaching: Proclaiming the Gospel against the Wisdom of the World* (Grand Rapids: Wm. B. Eerdmans Publishing Company, 1998).

186 Dorothee Söelle, *Suffering* (Philadelphia: Fortress Press, 1984).

187 Ronald Goetz, "The Suffering God: The Rise of a New Orthodoxy," *Christian Century* 103, no. 13 (1986).

188 Constantine is more formally referred to as Flavius Valerius Aurelius Constantinus.

189 Use of the term Christendom here refers to Christians worldwide as a collective body. Here it also points to a particular understanding that this worldview pervades understanding of all other aspects of life: political thinking, economic thinking, social thinking, and so on.

190 The *Lagerkapo* was a prisoner who was in charge of other prisoners. He acted as a sort of trustee.

191 Elie Weisel, *Night* (1972).

192 Ibid.

193 See Kurt Vonnegut, *Slaughterhouse-Five* (New York: Random House, Inc., 1969).

194 Matthew 8:17: "This was to fulfill what was spoken by the prophet Isaiah: 'He took our infirmities and bore our diseases.'" Dietrich Bonhoeffer, *Letters and Papers from Prison* (New York: MacMillan, 1962). Cf. Moltmann, *The Crucified God*.

195 Jeremiah 31:20: "Is Ephraim my dear son? Is he the child I delight in? As often as I speak against him, I still remember him. Therefore I am deeply moved for

him; I will surely have mercy on him, says the Lord." Kazoh Kitamori, *Theology of the Pain of God* (Louisville: John Knox Press, 1965).

196 Eberhard Jüngel, *God as the Mystery of the World: On the Foundation of the Theology of the Crucified One in the Dispute between Theism and Atheism* (Grand Rapids: Wm. B. Eerdmans Publishing Company, 1983).

197 *Oikonomia* is a Greek word that means the "law of the household," i.e., the way things should be with regard to everything in the master's domain. With regard to the Trinity, it refers to divine activity on behalf of the world. Catherine Mowry LaCugna, *God for Us* (San Francisco: HarperCollins Publishers, 1991).

198 David W. Lotz, "The Achievement of Jaroslav Pelikan," *First Things* 23, May (1992).Cf. Jaroslav Pelikan, *The Emergence of the Catholic Tradition (100-600)*, 5 vols., vol. 1 (Chicago: University of Chicago, 1971).

199 Abraham Joshua Heschel, *The Prophets* (New York: Harper & Row, 1972). Cf. Hosea 11:8-9, Jeremiah 31:20, etc.

200 Martin Marty, "Context," (February 15, 1994), 3.

201 Nils Alstrup Dahl, *The Crucified Messiah and Other Essays* (Minneapolis: Augsburg Publishing House, 1974).

202 "For God so loved the world that he gave his only Son, so that everyone who believes in him may not perish but may have eternal life."

203 Genesis 2:7: "The Lord formed man from the dust of the ground, and breathed into his nostrils the breath of life, and the man became a living being."

204 Ephesians 1:14: "This is the pledge of our inheritance toward redemption as God's own people, to the praise of his glory."

205 2 Corinthians 5:16-21. Cf. Romans 8:31-39.

206 John V. Taylor, *The Go-Between God: The Holy Spirit and the Christian Mission* (New York: Oxford University Press, 1979).

207 Jürgen Moltmann, *The Spirit of Life: A Universal Affirmation* (Minneapolis: Fortress Press, 1992).

208 Ibid.

209 Italics added. Ibid.

210 Harold Bloom, *The American Religion: The Emergence of the Post-Christian Nation* (New York: Simon & Schuster, 1992).

211 Arthur S. Sullivan, "I'm but a Stranger Here," in *The Lutheran Hymnal* (St. Louis: Concordia, 1836).

212 This is not the "supernaturalism" of the Greeks, which clearly divided the pure spiritual world and the impure material one. Rather, this Jewish, biblical worldview saw the two realms as equally real and having a great deal to do with each other.

213 The modern charismatic movement began in Van Nuys, California, in 1960 with Dennis Bennett. Michael Pollock Hamilton, *The Charismatic Movement* (Grand Rapids: Wm. B. Eerdmans Publishing Co., 1975).

214 Gerhard Ebeling, *The Nature of Faith*, trans. Ronald Gregor Smith (Philadelphia: Fortress Press, 1961).

215 Robert W. Jenson, *A Large Catechism* (Delhi, New York: American Lutheran Publicity Bureau, 1991).

216 Matthew 12:28: "If it is by the Spirit of God that I cast out demons, then the kingdom of God has come to you."

217 Luke 11:5-8: "And he said to them, 'Suppose one of you has a friend, and you go to him at midnight and say to him, "Friend, lend me three loaves of bread; for a friend of mine has arrived, and I have nothing to set before him." And he answers from within, "Do not bother me; the door has already been locked, and my children are with me in bed; I cannot get up and give you anything." I tell you, even though he will not get up and give him anything because he is his friend, at least because of his persistence he will get up and give him whatever he needs.'"

218 The Greek word is *parakletos*, which means "one called in to stand beside," or helper.

219 John 14:26.

220 Robert Jenson, "The Holy Spirit," in *Christian Dogmatics*, ed. Carl E. Braaten and Robert W. Jenson (Philadelphia: Fortress Press, 1984).

221 Ibid.

222 Ibid.

223 Moltmann, *The Spirit of Life: A Universal Affirmation*.

224 Ibid.

225 *Luther Works*, Vol. 31, 344

226 Gerhard Lohfink, *Jesus and Community: The Social Dimension of Christian Faith*, trans. John P. Galvin (Philadelphia: Fortress Press, 1984).

227 Jürgen Moltmann, *The Trinity and the Kingdom* (San Francisco: Harper and Row, Publishers, 1981).

228 All "articles" of the creeds are dimension of the one faith in the one Gospel and are not to be separated into "theologies." Still less can the three "persons" be separated from one another and re-imaged in more congenial "metaphors" or "models."

229 Martin E. Marty, *Noise of Conflict, 1919-1941*, vol. 2, Modern American Religion (Chicago: The University of Chicago Press, 1997).

230 Martin E. Marty, *A Nation of Behavers* (Chicago: The University of Chicago Press, 1976).

231 Robert N. Bellah et al., *Habits of the Heart* (Berkeley: University of California Press, 1985).

232 Italics are added. Ibid, 235.

233 Harold Bloom, *The American Religion*, and Philip J. Lee, *Against the Protestant Gnostics*, identify a number of characteristics associated with Gnosticism,

among them: 1) transcendence of God; 2) Jesus as mediator of the human individual and the unknowable God, with an emphasis on saving *knowledge*; 3) belief that saving knowledge is not universally accessible, but rather only to those to whom it is revealed through supernatural sources; the individual alone is competent to define salvation, revelation; 4) the historical Jesus is distorted through anachronistic projection, or through emphasis on "the Jesus of the Forty Days" (between the resurrection and the ascension); 5) individualistic, rather than corporate salvation; 6) indifference to, if not actual contempt for, the sacraments, especially the Eucharist as central to the gathering of the Christian church; 7) world-denying, rather than world-affirming, attitude; wants God to be "in control," to be a cosmic micro-manager of individual lives and destinies; 8) denial of "original sin" and the related practice of baptizing infants; says the individual has a divine quality or "spark," a "soul" which is eternal and which experiences a "fall" when it is born. Salvation is, in part, escape from the world; 9) emphasis in conversion on "technique;" 10) original Gnosticism had a profound anti-Jewish dimension; contemporary Gnosticism has an apocalyptic eschatology (expectation of the immanent end of the world) in which the restoration of the state of Israel plays a distinct role. Bloom, *The American Religion: The Emergence of the Post-Christian Nation* , Philip J. Lee, *Against the Protestant Gnostics* (New York: Oxford University Press, 1987).

234 Bloom, *The American Religion: The Emergence of the Post-Christian Nation.*

235 Sallie McFague, *Models of God: Theology for an Ecological, Nuclear Age* (Philadelphia: Fortress Press, 1987).

236 Isabel Carter Heyward, *The Redemption of God: A Theology of Mutual Relation* (New York: University Press of America, 1982).

237 The starting point for a systematic interpretation of Christian teachings determines two things: 1) how a particular account of Christianity is organized, and 2) which presuppositions will ground the argument (or apologetic case) upon which the relevant Christian claims will be made. In industrialized Western communities of the twenty-first century, a valid system will depend upon conceptualizations already established by scholars such as Plato, Aristotle, Descartes, Kant, Hegel, and Whitehead, for their theories are established as "givens" by persons who would be expected to hear the arguments being offered. The Scholastic model (or Medieval Scholasticism) understood theology two ways: first, in the literal sense as the doctrine of God, and secondly, as truth statements grounding the teachings of the church. Its origins derive from the Western Middle Ages—that is, about 1100 to 1500 A.D. Its proponents taught that while God's existence can be known from nature, only biblical revelation provides for full and complete knowledge of God. During this period, the *Summa theologica* written by Thomas Aquinas (1215-1274), with its dual reliance on natural theology (subject to human reason) and supernatural revelation (as interpreted in the church), provided the best description of this model. [Aquinas did not finish his *Summa theologica* before his death. However, from the text which is available, we can see that he intended to integrate Aristotelianism (the idea that one can argue by analogy from the natural

world to supernatural reality) into Christian thought. This approach is a contrast to Platonism, which claimed that the natural world is a mere shadow of supernatural realties.]

The beginning point for the Scholastic model is the inspiration of the Bible as the source for all theology—and more, as the norm for all knowledge. Its arguments (or apologetics) originated with these presuppositions. Once it is established that the Bible is God's inspired Word, all doctrine commences from that position. According to this model, then, Christian doctrine is defined as whatever the Bible teaches on a particular topic.

It is important to differentiate between scholastic theology and scholastic christology. Scholastic *theology* begins not with christology (the person of Christ), but with revelation, God, and the fall into sin. It addresses christology only as a preliminary to soteriology (the church's teaching on salvation—that is, the work of Christ). Moreover, scholastic *christology* does not begin with the history of Jesus (that is, "theology from below"), but with the divine *Logos* as the second person of the Holy Trinity (an approach which is known as "theology from above"). Only then does it introduce the historical Jesus, and does so by way of the incarnation; that is, its arguments rest on the claim that the *Logos* became "flesh" or "human" or "historical." Such assumptions assume that God's existence and attributes can be known from nature ("natural knowledge" or "natural theology") and that God's being as Holy Trinity can be derived from revelation.

The scholastic approach is "therapeutic" in that its purpose is to respond to the question of how humankind is to be redeemed after falling into sinfulness, and it is "restorative" in that it is concerned with God's will to correct a world that went wrong. Therefore, the Gospel is fundamentally a divine response to the sinful predicament of humanity.

Scholastic christology discloses the weaknesses and problems of christology "from above" in that its treatment of the "person of Christ" is disengaged from the Jewish historical matrix. That is, it requires an infusion of speculative architecture to relate the history of Jesus to the christological dogma. (Dogma arises whenever, in the course of prolonged controversy, it becomes clear that the truth of the Gospel is endangered. It defines something that belongs to the mandatory content of the Christian proclamation so that the Gospel is present in that proclamation. However, it is not the "law of believing" (*lex credendi*), but the "law of teaching" (*lex docendi*). That is, it determines what must be said by the church on a particular topic so that the Gospel happens in the church's proclamation and teaching. (When dogma is disengaged from the Gospel, it then becomes ideology, which carries with it oppressive and tyrannical attributes. The intention, by way of contrast, is to illuminate the evangelical or Gospel character of the church's message.) For example, assumptions about the nature of both God and human beings were ontological (supernatural being as the opposite of natural being) instead of historical, relational, and eschatological. This means that claims about God (for example, the claim that God is impassible) are not based on the Jewish context, but on a Hellenistic definition of God. Likewise, with regard to relationships, the human situation in association with God is one of differentiation, not one of humankind's sinful alienation. And finally, eschatological assumptions addressed not the future, or who or what determines the future; rather, they led to the denial of a worldview which would exclude the supernatural realm.

The problem with this model is that the appeal to specific biblical passages as the basis for arguing the authority of Scripture as the revealed Word of God is not an adequate basis for asserting claims about God among the general public. That is, among persons who do not already accept the legitimacy of Scripture, Scripture itself is not a compelling line of reasoning: it does not provide a foundation for why one should pay attention to Jesus.

Martin Luther (1483-1546) was critical of the scholastic model in the theses he penned in 1517. [See Martin Luther, "Disputation against Scholastic Theology," in *Luther's Works* (Philadelphia: Muhlenberg Press, 1957)]. Philip Melanchthon (1497-1560) revived this model, however, after Luther's death, and it survived as a method for understanding Lutheran theology for more than a century. (See my article on this topic: Walter R. Bouman, "Melanchthon's Significance for the Church Today," in *Philip Melanchthon Then and Now (1497-1997): Essays Celebrating the 500th Anniversary of the Birth of Philip Melanchthon, Theologian, Teacher and Reformer* (Columbia, South Carolina: Lutheran Theological Southern Seminary, 1999), 33-56. Its theological approach, method and content were reinstated again in the Protestant "Confessional Movement" of the nineteenth century, and they were reintroduced by Heinrich Schmid in 1843. [See Heinrich Schmid, *Der Dogmatik Der Evangelisch—Lutherischen Kirche*, 7th ed. (Gütersloh, Germany: Verlag Von C. Bertelsmann, 1893)]. However, as the scholastic model does not meet basic criteria for establishing the intelligibility of Christianity as the best answer for understanding the world, it is no longer appropriate. Alternatives to the Scholastic model are the creedal model, the law and gospel model, and the eschatological model. This text relies on the eschatological model for three reasons. First, is language is intelligible to both Christians and non-Christians; secondly, it offers credible reasons for the claim that Jesus is the Messiah; and finally, it provides reasonable coherence as to an understanding of reality through acceptance of the Christian story.

238 Oliver O'Donovan, *The Resurrection and Moral Order: An Outline for Evangelical Ethics* (Grand Rapids: Wm. B. Eerdmans Publishing Company, 1994).

239 Jenson, *A Large Catechism*.

240 Moltmann, *The Spirit of Life: A Universal Affirmation*.

241 Modalism (also called modalistic monarchianism) claimed that the Father, the Son, and the Spirit are three modes or manifestations of the one God. Its supporter was Sabellius (ca. 215 A.D.), who taught that God appeared in a succession of roles or acted in a variety of ways, first as creator (manifest especially in Israel), then as redeemer (manifest notably in the life of Jesus),

and then as sanctifier (God's peculiar way of being in the church). This understanding of the Trinity (enjoying some popularity again today) concerns God's actions in relation to the world. It treats the three persons of the Trinity as masks that God could take off and put on. Because it overlooks the biblical witness that the God of Israel creates and the Second Person of the Trinity saves, and because it does not deal with the relationship of the three persons to each other, this view was and is rejected as heretical.

242 Some questions may be posed as to whether the accent should be on God's uniqueness or God's exclusivity. The NRSV gives four possible translations, and the answer is probably that both accents are involved. George Arthur Buttrick, *Interpreter's Dictionary of the Bible*, vol. IV (Nashville: Abingdon Press, 1962).

BIBLIOGRAPHY

Abelard, Peter. "Exposition of the Epistle to the Romans." In *A Scholastic Miscellany: Anselm to Ockham*. Philadelphia: The Westminster Press, 1956.

Alighieri, Dante. *Divine Comedy: Inferno, Purgatory, Paradise*. Vol. Canto XXXIII. New York: Everyman's Library, 1995.

Arendt, Hannah. *On Revolution*. 10th ed. New York: The Viking Press, Inc., 1970.

Athanasius. *The Incarnation of the Word of God*. New York: Macmillan, 1954.

Aulén, Gustaf. *Christus Victor: An Historical Study of the Three Main Types of Atonement*. Translated by A. G. Hebert. London: SPCK, 1950.

Bellah, Robert N., Richard Madsen, William M. Sullivan, Ann Swidler, and Steven M. Tipton. *Habits of the Heart*. Berkeley: University of California Press, 1985.

Berne, Eric. *What Do You Say after Hello?* New York: Bantam Books, 1973.

Bloom, Harold. *The American Religion: The Emergence of the Post-Christian Nation* New York: Simon & Schuster, 1992.

Bonhoeffer, Dietrich. *Letters and Papers from Prison*. New York: MacMillan, 1962.

Bornkamm, Güenther. *Jesus of Nazareth*. Translated by Irene and Fraser McLuskey with James M. Robinson. New York: Harper & Row, Publishers, 1960.

Bornkamm, Günther. *The New Testament: A Guide to Its Writings*. Philadelphia: Fortress Press, 1973.

Bouman, Walter R. "Faith Sustains and Comforts as End of This Life Draws Near." *The Columbus Dispatch*, June 17 2005.

———. "Melanchthon's Significance for the Church Today." In *Philip Melanchthon Then and Now (1497-1997): Essays Celebrating the 500th Anniversary of the Birth of Philip Melanchthon, Theologian, Teacher and Reformer*. Columbia, SC: Lutheran Theological Southern Seminary, 1999.

Braaten, Carl. "Locus 6." In *Christian Dogmatics*, 1984.

Buttrick, George Arthur. *Interpreter's Dictionary of the Bible*. Vol. IV. Nashville: Abingdon Press, 1962.

———, ed. *Psalms of Solomon*, 4 vols. Vol. 3, The Interpreter's Bictionary of the Bible. Nashville: Abingdon Press, 1962.

Campenhausen, Hans Von. "The Events of Easter and the Empty Tomb." In *Tradition and Life in the Church*.

Capon, Robert Farrar. *Hunting the Divine Fox: Images and Mystery in Christian Faith*. New York: The Seabury Press, 1974.

———. *Kingdom, Grace, Judgment: Paradox, Outrage, and Vindication in the Parables of Jesus*. Combined Ed. ed. Grand Rapids: Wm. B. Eerdmans Publishing Company, 2002.

———. *The Foolishness of Preaching: Proclaiming the Gospel against the Wisdom of the World*. Grand Rapids: Wm. B. Eerdmans Publishing Company, 1998.

Capra, Frank. "It's a Wonderful Life." US: Liberty Films (II), 1947.

Carroll, Robert P. "Israel, History of (Post-Monarchic Period)." In *Anchor Bible Dictionary*, edited by David Noel Freedman. New York: Doubleday, 1992.

Crossan, John Dominic. *The Dark Interval: Toward a Theology of Story*.

Dahl, Nils Alstrup. *The Crucified Messiah and Other Essays*. Minneapolis: Augsburg Publishing House, 1974.

Dr. Martin Luther's Large Catechism. Translated by J. N. Lenker. Minneapolis: Augsburg Publishing House, 1935.

Dunn, James D.G. "Pharisees, Sinners, and Jesus." In *The Social World of Formative Christianity and Judaism: Essays in Tribute to Howard Clark Kee*, edited by Richard Horsley. Philadelphia: Fortress Press, 1988.

———. *The Evidence for Jesus*. Louisville: The Westminster Press, 1985.

Ebeling, Gerhard. *The Nature of Faith*. Translated by Ronald Gregor Smith. Philadelphia: Fortress Press, 1961.

Fasching, Darrell J. *The Coming of the Millennium: Good News for the Whole Human Race*. Lincoln, NE: Authors Choice Press, 2001.

Forde, Gerhard. *Theology Is for Proclamation*. Minneapolis: Augsburg Fortress, 1990.

Forde, Gerhard O. "The Work of Christ." In *Christian Dogmatics*, edited by Carl E. Braaten and Robert W. Jenson. Philadelphia: Fortress Press, 1984.

Fortunatus, Venantius Honorius. "Welcome, Happy Morning." In *Lutheran Book of Worship*. Minneapolis: Augsburg Publishing House, 1996.

Goetz, Ronald. "The Suffering God: The Rise of a New Orthodoxy." *Christian Century* 103, no. 13 (1986): 385-89.

Gollwitzer, Helmut. *The Dying and Living Lord*. Philadelphia: Muhlenberg Press 1960.

Hall, Douglas John. *Lighten Our Darkness: Toward an Indigenous Theology of the Cross*. Philadelphia: The Westminster Press, 1976.

Hamilton, Michael Pollock. *The Charismatic Movement*. Grand Rapids: Wm. B. Eerdmans Publishing Co., 1975.

Hauerwas, Stanley. *Truthfulness and Tragedy: Further Investigations into Christian Ethics*. Notre Dame, Indiana: University of Notre Dame Press, 1977.

Havergal, Frances R. "Lord, Speak to Us, That We May Speak " In *Lutheran Book of Worship*. Minneapolis: Augsburg Publishing House, 1996.

Hawking, Stephen. *A Brief History of Time: A Reader's Companion*. New York: Bantam, 1992.

Heermann, Johann. "Ah, Holy Jesus." In *Lutheran Book of Worship*. Minneapolis: Augsburg Publishing House, 1996.

Hengel, Martin. *Between Jesus and Paul: Studies in the Earliest History of Christianity*. Eugene, OR: Wipf & Stock Publishers, 2003.

———. *Crucifixion*. Philadelphia: Fortress Press, 1977.

Heschel, Abraham Joshua. *The Prophets*. New York: Harper & Row, 1972.

Heyward, Isabel Carter. *The Redemption of God: A Theology of Mutual Relation*. New York: University Press of America, 1982.

Hultgren, Arland J. *Christ and His Benefits: Christology and Redemption in the New Testament*. Philadelphia: Fortress Press, 1987.

Irenaeus. *Irenaeus against Heresies*. Whitefish, MT: Kessinger Publishing, 2004.

Iwand, H. J. "Christologievollesung (Unpublished)."

Jenson, Robert. "The Holy Spirit." In *Christian Dogmatics*, edited by Carl E. Braaten and Robert W. Jenson. Philadelphia: Fortress Press, 1984.

Jenson, Robert W. *A Large Catechism*. Delhi, NY: American Lutheran Publicity Bureau, 1991.

———. "How the World Lost Its Story." *First Things* (1993).

———. "The Last Judgment." *Ad Fontes*.

———. "The Triune God." In *Christian Dogmatics*, edited by Carl E. Braaten. Philadelphia: Fortress Press, 1984.

Jeremias, Joachim. *The Parables of Jesus*. Translated by S. H. Hooke. New York: SCM Press Ltd., 1963.

Jüngel, Eberhard. *God as the Mystery of the World: On the Foundation of the Theology of the Crucified One in the Dispute between Theism and Atheism*. Grand Rapids: Wm. B. Eerdmans Publishing Company, 1983.

Kant, Immanuel. "Critique of Pure Reason." In *The Cambridge Edition of the Works of Immanuel Kant*, edited by Paul Guyer and Allen W. Wood. New York: Cambridge University Press, 1999.

Kitamori, Kazoh. *Theology of the Pain of God*. Louisville: John Knox Press, 1965.

LaCugna, Catherine Mowry. *God for Us*. San Francisco: HarperCollins Publishers, 1991.

Lapide, Pinchas. *The Resurrection of Jesus: A Jewish Perspective*. Minneapolis: Augsburg Publishing House, 1983.

Lee, Philip J. *Against the Protestant Gnostics*. New York: Oxford University Press, 1987.

Lewis, C.S. *Beyond Personality: The Christian Idea of God*. New York: The Macmillan Co., 1945.

Lohfink, Gerhard. *Jesus and Community: The Social Dimension of Christian Faith*. Translated by John P. Galvin. Philadelphia: Fortress Press, 1984.

Lotz, David W. "The Achievement of Jaroslav Pelikan." *First Things* 23, May (1992): 55-65.

Luther, Martin. "Disputation against Scholastic Theology." In *Luther's Works*. Philadelphia: Muhlenberg Press, 1957.

Macdougall, Allan Ross, ed. *Letters of Edna St. Vincent Millay*. New York: Harper & Brothers, Publishers, 1952.

Marty, Martin E. "Context." Feb. 15, 1994.

————. *Noise of Conflict, 1919-1941*. Vol. 2, Modern American Religion. Chicago: The University of Chicago Press, 1997.

————. *A Nation of Behavers*. Chicago: The University of Chicago Press, 1976.

Masius, John. In *Touched by an Angel*. US: 20th Century Fox, 1994.

Masters, Edgar Lee. *Spoon River Anthology*. New York: The Macmillan Company, 1915.

McClurkin, Donnie. "Lord, I Lift Your Name on High." In *Live in London and More*, 4:22, 2000.

McFague, Sallie. *Models of God: Theology for an Ecological, Nuclear Age*. Philadelphia: Fortress Press, 1987.

Moltmann, Jürgen. *The Crucified God*. Translated by R.A. Wilson and John Bowden. 1st U.S. ed. New York: SCM Press Ltd., 1974.

————. *The Spirit of Life: A Universal Affirmation*. Minneapolis: Fortress Press, 1992.

————. *The Way of Jesus Christ: Christology in Messianic Dimensions*. Translated by Margaret Kohl. New York: HarperCollins Publishers, 1993.

————. *The Trinity and the Kingdom*. San Francisco: Harper and Row, Publishers, 1981.

————. *Theology of Hope: On the Ground and the Implications of a Christian Eschatology*. New York: Harper & Row, Publishers, 1967.

O'Collins, G.S.J. *Jesus Risen: An Historical, Fundamental and Systematic Examination of Christ's Resurrection*. New York: Paulist Press, 1987.

O'Donovan, Oliver. *The Resurrection and Moral Order: An Outline for Evangelical Ethics*. Grand Rapids: Wm. B. Eerdmans Publishing Company, 1994.

Oden, Thomas C. *The Structure of Awareness*. Nashville: Abingdon Press, 1969.

Pannenberg, Wolfhart. *An Introduction to Systematic Theology*. Grand Rapids: Wm. B. Eerdmans Publishing Company, 1991.

————. *Theology and the Kingdom of God*. Philadelphia: Westminster John Knox Press, 1969.

Pearsall, Judy, and Bill Trumble, eds. *The Oxford Encyclopedic English Dictionary*. 2nd ed. New York: Oxford University Press, 1995.

Pelikan, Jaroslav. *The Emergence of the Catholic Tradition (100-600)*. 5 vols. Vol. 1. Chicago: University of Chicago, 1971.

Powell, Mark Allan. *Fortress Introduction to the Gospels*. Minneapolis: Augsburg Fortress, 1998.

Russell, Bertrand. *A History of Western Philosophy*. New York: Simon & Schuster, 1972.

Schmid, Heinrich. *Der Dogmatik Der Evangelisch - Lutherischen Kirche*. 7th ed. Gütersloh, Germany: Verlag Von C. Bertelsmann, 1893.

Schwarz, Hans. *Eschatology*. Grand Rapids: Wm. B. Eerdmans Publishing Company, 2001.

————. *On the Way to the Future: A Christian View of Eschatology in the Light of Current Trends in Religion, Philosophy, and Science*. Minneapolis: Augsburg Publishing, 1972.

Smith, Robert. *Easter Gospels*. Minneapolis: Augsburg Publishing House, 1983.

Smith, Robert H. *The Easter Gospels: The Resurrection of Jesus According to the Four Evangelists*. Minneapolis: Augsburg Publishing House, 1983.

Söelle, Dorothee. *Suffering*. Philadelphia: Fortress Press, 1984.

Stendahl, Krister, ed. *Immortality and Resurrection*. New York: Macmillan, 1965.

Sullivan, Arthur S. "I'm but a Stranger Here." In *The Lutheran Hymnal*. St. Louis: Concordia, 1836.

Taylor, John V. *The Go-Between God: The Holy Spirit and the Christian Mission*. New York: Oxford University Press, 1979.

The Loci Communes of Philipp Melanchthon. Translated by Charles L. Hill. Boston: Meador Publishing Co., 1944.

Thielicke, Helmut. *Death and Life*. Translated by Edward H. Schroeder. Philadelphia: Fortress Press, 1970.

Tillich, Paul. *Dynamics of Faith*. New York: Harper & Row, Publishers, Inc., 1957.

Updike, John. *Telephone Poles and Other Poems*. 1st ed. New York: Alfred A. Knopf, 1963.

Vonnegut, Kurt. *Slaughterhouse-Five*. New York: Random House, Inc., 1969.

Weisel, Elie. *Night*, 1972.

Wills, Garry. *Lincoln at Gettysburg: The Words That Remade America*. New York: Touchtone, 1992.

Wright, N. T. *The Challenge of Jesus: Rediscovering Who Jesus Was and Is*. Downers Grove, Illinois: InterVarsity Press, 1999.

————. *The Resurrection of the Son of God*. 5 vols. Vol. 3, Christian Origins and the Question of God. Minneapolis: Fortress Press, 2003.

————. *Jesus and the Victory of God*. 5 vols. Vol. 2, Christian Origins and the Question of God. Minneapolis: Fortress Press, 1996.

————. *The Challenge of Jesus: Rediscovering Who Jesus Was and Is*: InterVarsity Press, 1999.

————. *The New Testament and the People of God*. 5 vols. Vol. 1, Christian Origins and the Question of God. Minneapolis: Fortress Press, 1992.